CREDIT REPAIR

Guide for Credit Repair and to Increase the Score
to Get a Good Business Profile

(The Fastest Way to Increase Your Credit Score
With a Few Easy Steps)

Kevin Teachout

Published by Knowledge Icons

Kevin Teachout

All Rights Reserved

Credit Repair: Guide for Credit Repair and to Increase the Score to Get a Good Business Profile (The Fastest Way to Increase Your Credit Score With a Few Easy Steps)

ISBN 978-1-990084-76-8

Legal & Disclaimer

The information contained in this book is not designed to replace or take the place of any form of medicine or professional medical advice. The information in this book has been provided for educational and entertainment purposes only.

The information contained in this book has been compiled from sources deemed reliable, and it is accurate to the best of the Author's knowledge; however, the Author cannot guarantee its accuracy and validity and cannot be held liable for any errors or omissions. Changes are periodically made to this book. You must consult your doctor or get professional medical advice before using any of the suggested remedies, techniques, or information in this book.

TABLE OF CONTENTS

Introduction

First and foremost, thank you and congratulations for purchasing this book and making the decision to take responsibility for your financial future.

Every day millions of Americans worry about how they will pay their rent next month, if the check they wrote yesterday will bounce today, and if they will be able to buy their kids new shoes, clothes and school supplies. They simply haven't learned ways to manage their money that will reduce these worries and put them on track to financial well-being.

This book will give you the foundation to begin planning for your financial future. It was written for the average person who lives paycheck to paycheck and doesn't see a way off the financial hamster wheel and out of debt. It is for those who don't believe they make enough to save, who feel that it's normal to struggle to make ends meet.

If that's not you, and you already have your finances in order, then you might already know most of the information presented in this book. But for those who are just beginning to think about their financial futures, those who want to start saving to make that big purchase or who are just thinking about college for their kids, please read on.

Chapter 1: Check Your Credit Report For Any Errors And Dispute Them

The first and foremost thing to do is to request a free credit report from major credit bureaus and check for any errors and dispute them. Currently, there are three major credit reference agencies operating in the US:

• Experian- 1 888 397 3742 /http://www.experian.com

• Equifax- 1-888-202-4025 / http://www.equifax.com

• TransUnion- 877-322-8228 / http://www.transunion.com

You are legally entitled to obtain a free credit report once in 12 months, so the best you can do is to take advantage of this opportunity and go through your credit report to see if there are any errors. Errors do show up on your credit report such as incorrect credit limits, any late payments or collection items that were not done by you.

Typical Errors You Need To Check In Your Credit Report:

• Personal Information - errors in your mailing address or date of birth

• Financial Transactions - any errors on your credit card or loan accounts. Watch out for errors in payment dates.

• Identity Theft – you need to immediately report to your credit agency in case you find signs of identity theft such as new loans or credit cards listed that you have not opened yourself.

How Do I Dispute Errors Found In My Credit Report?

☐ STEP 1: the first thing you need to do is to contact your credit reporting company in writing and inform them about the errors found on your credit report. Include any documents or copies that support your argument. Make sure that you state your correct name and address along with the item you wish to dispute in your report. Clearly explain with supporting facts why you want to dispute the information and request them to remove it from your report.

☐ STEP 2: if you think you are a victim to identity theft, you should inform your local police and file a complaint with them. This should be done prior to contacting your credit agency, because the CRA will require a copy of the complaint with your local police.

It usually takes 30 to 90 days for credit reporting companies to investigate your dispute and remove data from your credit report. Once it is removed, credit reporting companies send you a letter with a free copy of your report confirming the change. The faster you act on your errors, the easier it becomes for you to boost your credit score.

Chapter 2: What Is Your Credit Score?

Poor credit can be an embarrassment to you and your family. You may have grown up in a family where poor credit was the norm and you just accept it as your norm. Many people with credit or financial difficulties tend to ignore their financial problems. You might be simply biding your time, like many people with poor credit, waiting for those blemishes to fall off your credit report. In most case this will take seven years from the date of inclusion.

BUT BURYING YOUR HEAD IN THE SAND, LIKE AN OSTRICH, IS THE BIGGEST MISTAKE YOU CAN MAKE.

What you probably don't know is that no credit can be worse than poor credit. So if you are simply waiting and hoping that your credit problems will just disappear in seven years, WRONG! You need to improving your credit, which requires proactive steps. Otherwise, you will be saddled with bad credit even after your disparaging items fall off your report.

Credit scores can increase significantly in as little as two months and most people will see huge increases within two years, just by being proactive. But if you do nothing, your score will remain poor for at least seven years, and in all probability longer than that.

Many individuals think a poor financial record is a sign of poor character, and the task of dealing with it might seem overwhelming. Be assured that bad credit and financial issues happen to all types of people, in all walks of life. Both Walt Disney, Mark Twain claimed bankruptcy and Donald Trump more than once. In many situations it occurs because of a crisis, a job loss, a divorce, or sudden illness. But let's not forget, one of the major reasons it happens, is because we make irresponsible and rash decisions concerning our finances, or because we just mismanage our money.

Let's just leave it in the past. You should start adopting proactive steps to take control of your credit score. It all starts by knowing your credit score, but please use caution where you obtain your credit score.

Obtaining Your Credit Score From the Wrong Source

Let's be honest, you cannot take control of your credit score if you do not know what your score is. While you might be proactively downloading your score from Internet sites, you may not be looking at the actual score a lender will see. Obtaining your credit score from the wrong source can give you a false sensitivity of your credit standing.

The credit-scoring world is complicated and cloaked in mystery. In fact, your credit score **will be** different depending on who asks for your score and where the credit report is being reported. If you have ever pulled your credit report from the big three (Equifax, Experian or TransUnion) you have seen the different scores each source reports.

Now, if a Bank or Credit Card Company asks for your score, the score will be a very different number than from the score you see when you ask for your own score. There's a simple reason for this, because the primary credit reporting bureaus modify the formula according to the person or company "pulling" the credit report. An automobile company is more interested your payment history for installment loans than a landlord who is more interest in your payment history in general. Because of the different needs of the parties pulling the credit report, the credit bureaus apply four different formulas to determine your score, depending on who is asking for your score.

Here are the four different categories:

☐ Consumer- The score you see when you pull a credit report.

☐ Auto The score installment payment lenders see when they pull your credit report.

☐ Tenant – The score the potential Landlord sees when they pull your credit report.

☐ FICO– The score Lenders and credit card companies see when they pull your credit report.

The CONSUMER FORMULA is plain and simple; it's used when you request your own credit score. In most cases, this score is significantly higher than the FICO score. Automobile loans are based on the AUTO FORMULA which is the score lenders use to determine whether to grant you an automobile loan or installment loans. The TENANT FORMULA is used by landlords considering whether to rent to you or not. Finally, the FICO Score is the score lenders and credit card companies use to decide whether to extend to you a home loan, credit card, or line of credit. The FICO Score is the most important of all the scores; it usually is the lowest score and holds the most weight with lenders.

Consequently, if you purchase your own credit score online, it definitely will not be the same score seen by lenders. Alternatively, you will see your consumer score, which will apt be higher than the score the lenders see. It has been tested with different credit score levels and found to be as much as 30-point differences between the consumer score and the FICO score on the same day.

So now you can see that your score changes based on who is reporting it and who is requesting it. The three major credit bureaus – TransUnion, Equifax, and Experian – are responsible for monitoring credit activity and reporting credit scores. Conversely, not all creditors provide information to each bureau. This in turn means that each bureau will normally report a different score. Despite the fact, that not all information on the reports is updated diligently by bureaus when they are given information, accounts for more differences in their scores.

You as a consumer need to go find your accurate FICO credit scores. This score does not fall into the government's free credit report program, so you will have to purchase it. One of the best sources to obtain your FICO score is to go to www.myfico.com and purchase your credit report.

Paying Bills That Are In Collections

It just seems logical that if you pay a bill in collection, your credit score will increase. If you look at this from a CREDIT perspective, paying a bill that has been turned over for collection can be more damaging than ignoring it.

Your recent payment history is far more important than your older past payment history. The formulas for collection accounts only minimally affect your score after two years. In fact they are almost erased after four years. So, every time you make a payment on a collection account, that payment renews the activity. Thus damaging your credit score and it restarts the seven year period in which the item remains on your credit report. Also in some states, payments restart the statue of limitations on when the creditors can sue you for the debt.

With that being said, paying a bill in collection is ALWAYS the right thing to do. It is your debt and your responsibility to pay your debts. So what should you do about the debt?

Prior to paying a debt in collection you should negotiate with the collection agent. You might be able to get the collection account deleted from credit report entirely. This may involve paying the debt in full with one payment or some lesser agreed upon amount with the collection agent. Negotiate with them; some money is better than no money plus the cost litigation. They also get the additional tax break on the chargeoff for the amount not paid.

Chapter 3: The Components Of A Credit Report

This chapter is written to give a thorough explanation of a credit report and how it reads. The primary sections of a credit bureau are that I mainly look at are:

☐ Identification

☐ Credit scores

☐ Public Records

☐ Mortgage History

☐ Non-Derogatory Trade lines

☐ Derogatory Trade lines

☐ Closed accounts

☐ Inquiries

☐ Complete Trade line Summary

Let's look at the first section on a credit report which is:

Identification

The first section of all credit reports is the identification of the applicant and the company that ordered the credit report.

Next going down on the left is the applicant and co-applicant's name, social security number, marital status, current address and previous address.

On the right is the date of the credit report. VERY IMPORTANT

Below the date are the 3 credit reporting companies reporting. XP represents Experian, TU represents TransUnion and EF represents Equifax. These are the three repositories that compose this tri-merge credit report.

The next section we will show the three credit scores on a credit report.

Credit Scores

Credit scores were designed to prevent bankruptcy. Due to high credit card debts excellent paying customers found themselves better off bankrupting credit card debts. This created FICO scoring system. It not only tracks how well you pay but it also tracks how close you are to your total credit limit.

The closer you are to your total limit the lower the score. That's the rules of FICO.

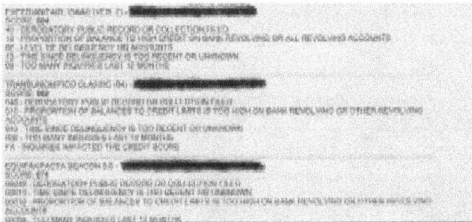

On this credit report, the Experian credit score is the highest with a 684, next comes the TransUnion score of 682 and finally the lowest score is 674.

The middle score is the primary score in the mortgage world.

Credit scores range from a low of 350 to a high of 850, the higher the score the better the credit. This score would be considered a "B."

Here is another example of credit scores. This credit bureau's middle score is 617. Some FHA lenders allow a low 620 middle score, but most want a minimum score of 640 or higher to qualify.

In later chapters I'll explain quick little fixes that can raise these credit scores quickly.

EXPERIAN/FAIR, ISAAC (VER. 2) -
SCORE: 646
38 - SERIOUS DELINQUENCY AND PUBLIC RECORD OR COLLECTION FILED
20 - TIME SINCE DEROGATORY PUBLIC RECORD OR COLLECTION IS TOO SHORT
10 - PROPORTION OF BALANCE TO HIGH CREDIT ON BANK REVOLVING OR ALL REVOLVING ACCOUNTS
18 - NUMBER OF ACCOUNTS WITH DELINQUENCY
08 - TOO MANY INQUIRIES LAST 12 MONTHS

TRANSUNION/FICO CLASSIC (04) -
SCORE: 617
038 - SERIOUS DELINQUENCY, AND PUBLIC RECORD OR COLLECTION FILED
026 - LENGTH OF TIME SINCE DEROGATORY PUBLIC RECORD OR COLLECTION IS TOO SHORT
010 - PROPORTION OF BALANCES TO CREDIT LIMITS IS TOO HIGH ON BANK REVOLVING OR OTHER REVOLVING
ACCOUNTS
013 - TIME SINCE DELINQUENCY IS TOO RECENT OR UNKNOWN
FA - INQUIRIES IMPACTED THE CREDIT SCORE

EQUIFAX/FACTA BEACON 5.0 -
SCORE: 609
00038 - SERIOUS DELINQUENCY, AND DEROGATORY PUBLIC RECORD OR COLLECTION FILED
00013 - TIME SINCE DELINQUENCY IS TOO RECENT OR UNKNOWN
00018 - NUMBER OF ACCOUNTS WITH DELINQUENCY
00010 - PROPORTION OF BALANCES TO CREDIT LIMITS IS TOO HIGH ON BANK REVOLVING OR OTHER REVOLVING
ACCOUNTS
FA - NUMBER OF INQUIRIES ADVERSELY AFFECTED THE SCORE, BUT NOT SIGNIFICANTLY

Public Records

Public records on credit reports show legal proceedings including bankruptcies, foreclosures, federal tax liens, state tax liens, judgments, child support and repossessions.

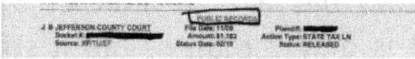

Above is a small state tax lien for illustration purposes. This lien has been released. The filing date, the county it was filed in, the dollar amount and the lien status are all standard on a credit report.

Mortgage History

Next on a credit report is mortgage history. All credit reports list the mortgages separate from other accounts. Below I show you how to read a mortgage history on a credit bureau.

The two accounts above are different mortgage histories. The top one last reported on 1/13; account opened in 11/12 and has a high limit of $218762. Since it is only 2 months old it still has a balance of 218762. It is a 30 year mortgage with payments of $1557 per month.

The second one reads the same except it has original balance of $65,600 now the balance is $58037. The payments are $520 per month and both mortgages are paid as agreed.

Next on all credit report is a listing of all good paying accounts called Non-Derogatory accounts.

If Capital One balance could drop below $250 this credit score could go up 15 points or higher.

Derogatory Accounts

Derogatory accounts are bad paying accounts that have late payments, collections and charged-off creditors.

Collection #1 is a nice size collection account that opened in 3/07. This account can be removed on 3/14. Accounts #2 and 3 are both newer medical collections.

Closed Accounts

Credit reports also list paid off accounts on a credit bureau. A paid off or closed account shows the type of loans you borrowed in the past.

Inquiries

Inquiries will show companies that pulled your credit report within a given period of time. This credit report only list inquiries within the last 120 days.

Trade Summary

The trade section is where you can get a synopsis of all your trades and debts. This valuable information can be used for credit repair because it lists all revolving debts, collections, late payments and public records.

	TRADE SUMMARY				
	#	BALANCE	HIGH CREDIT	PAYMENTS	PAST DUE
MORTGAGE	6	276709	264382	2077	0
AUTO	1	0	0	0	0
EDUCATION	0	0	0	0	0
OTHER INSTALLMENT	0	0	0	0	0
OPEN	5	1042	8976	1042	0
REVOLVING	24	24631	82444	628	0
OTHER	0	0	0	0	0
TOTAL	39	302472	343782	3747	0

SECURED DEBT	58037	OLDEST TRADELINE	09/82
UNSECURED DEBT	244435	DEBT/HIGH CREDIT	88%

DEROGATORY SUMMARY

CHARGE OFFS:	0	30 DAYS:	3	INQUIRIES:	5
COLLECTIONS:	0	60 DAYS:	1	MOST RECENT LATE: 07/12	
BANKRUPTCY:	0	90 DAYS:	0		
PUBLIC RECORDS:	1	OTHER:	0		

EQUIFAX IDENTITY SCAN

Finally we come to the creditors section of the credit bureau.

This is where you can find the addresses and phone numbers of all creditors reporting on your account. You will also find the address and phone numbers of the 3 credit reporting agencies.

Now let's look at some credit reports that we can use as a case study for credit repair.

Disputing credit bureaus can be very time consuming. Also the credit bureaus are not stupid when it comes to dispute letters. They have the right to ignore frivolous credit disputes. If at all possible I highly recommend you consider using a professional service that knows the rules and how to operate within the law.

Credit Report -Repair Analysis #1

Imagine this is you and your wife's credit report and we are looking at your credit report on my computer screen.

First you'd notice the date of the report at the top (10/25/12).

Then I would explain your credit scores. The Three scores at the top are yours (Husband). The next three scores are your wife's. Also notice that you (husband) only have 2 scores, while your wife has the normal three credit scores.

I have highlighted your middle score which is the primary score. It only registers a score of 515. On the scale of 350-850, your score is too low for a FHA mortgage loan.

Your credit score would be considered a "D."

Beneath your scores are your wife's credit scores. Her scores are not much better. Her middle score is 588. She is also a "D."

In order to understand why these scores are so low we need to examine your whole credit report and look for credit inaccuracies and make use of the FCRA laws to improve your credit rating.

If you are doing this at home get out your magnifying glass and look at every trade-line listed on your credit bureau. I am almost certain that you can find something in error, even if it is just the account number.

The next page on your credit bureau is the Public Records Section. Let's examine it for accuracy.

Credit Reporting on Public Records

As you can see, you and your wife have a lot of liens and judgments. But, remember rule number 2? Collections and negative items can only remain on a credit report for 7 years with the exception of bankruptcy.

So I have numbered all the filing dates on these liens and have discovered that 4 of these liens can be removed. Also one is a bankruptcy that is 8 years old.

You can dispute them yourself but I would certainly consider a credit repair service because they are the experts in challenging credit reports. Not only can they remove these out dated ones, but disputes for inaccuracy could be made for all these public record accounts.

Removal of these records would certainly help both of your credit scores and it would clean up a junky looking credit report.

On the next page of your credit report we look at the mortgage section and paid as agreed accounts.

Mortgage Reporting on Your Credit Report

Page 4 of your credit report lists your mortgage history first.

As you can see in section 1 there are no late payments in last 12 months on your mortgage. However, the previous 12 months does record late payments and these negative payments can affect your credit scores.

It wouldn't hurt to dispute these late payments. They may get removed and increase your credit rating and scores.

In section 2 the three credit agencies record all your good paying accounts as Non-Derogatory accounts.

Capital One credit card has a high limit of $500 and the balance is $335. To increase credit scores and credit rating, pay down balances on all credit cards below 50% of credit limit, in this instance $250.

This technique works for good credit people too. I once raised a man's credit score from 620 to 740 just by transferring balances and raising credit limits on all his credit cards.

Section 3 of your credit report is the beginning of derogatory accounts that begin with late payments and collections.

Since there are six pages of collections I will only use one to illustrate how your collections read on a credit report.

Many people think that paying off a collection solves the problem.

But I remember when an applicant was trying to raise a credit score and thought paying off a collection would boost the score. It didn't boost the credit score at all. In fact it actually lowered the credit scores. I think it has something to do with a new collection date.

Now based on this credit report and credit scores you are not eligible for a FHA mortgage at this time. Also FHA will only allow up to $1000 in collections before they will approve a mortgage loan.

But don't despair; the good news is credit reports like this one can get cleaned up within a year using FCRA and a good credit repair specialist.

Let's recap this credit report and analyze the credit repair that can be used to increase your credit rating.

Credit Report – Credit Repair Recap

☐You have a very low credit score because of accurate andinaccurate items being reported by the 3 credit reporting agencies.

☐You have a good 12 month mortgage history but your credit bureau reports 30 day late payments in the last 24 months. These late payments could affect your credit bureau and credit scores negatively.

☐You and your wife have 3 "good paying" accounts but only one is active and it has a balance that needs lowering to boost credit scores.

☐I also would advise that you both begin to establish more positive accounts by possibly getting several accounts established. If you cannot get any unsecured credit then I would use secured credit cards to boost your credit score.

☐An installment loan that reports to all 3 credit agencies could go a long way to help both credit reports and credit scores.

☐Finally your collections, late payments and charged-off accounts make your credit bureau look cluttered. Start immediately to dispute these old outdated public records and collections.

I know this client is not you, but he and his wife are real people and this is the exact conversation I had with them. I hope they follow through because they are good people.

Their credit report is a good example to illustrate the work it takes to fix a credit report and how to use the FCRA laws to erase a bad credit bureau and build a "good credit report."

Now let's look at another credit report that we can examine to repair.

As you can see this credit report also has low credit scores.I chose this credit report to show what can be done to improve credit scores.

Notice the writing in parenthesis. Even the credit bureau itself emphasizes that incorrect, inaccurate, outdated or missing info can be used to raise credit scores and improve a credit report.

This is page 2 of his credit bureau and once again it lists his credit scores.However, his public records are what I want you to see.

FHA allows bankruptcy to be over 2 years before you can qualify for a mortgage loan. Even though he has 3 listed bankruptcies, they are all over 2 years old so they cannot be used against him.

On page 3 is where his credit scores can be raised. Look at his non-derogatory accounts and see the potential to raise his credit scores.

There are three good paying accounts that he can use to raise his credit scores.

Credit one bank's balance needs to drop down below 50% of his credit limit. Also Leroy's Jewelers and First premier's balances need to be paid down below the 50% threshold.

By doing this I am sure he will increase his scores at least 40 points.

The last account is the best account. It has a credit limit of $600 but he only owes

35

$216 on it. If he had all his accounts at this level of the high credit limit his scores would already be higher!

These are small fixes for a major purchase that he wants to make.

Page 4 lists all his derogatory accounts. As you can see all he has are collections. FHA allows up to $1000 in collections and he has just over $400. This credit report is can be repaired quickly and qualify for anFHA loan.

Now let's recap this credit report for ways to increase his credit scores and buy a home .

Credit Report- Credit Score Analysis# 2

☐He has a low credit score of 597 (middle score) and needs to increase his scores 43 points or higher.

☐He has 3 bankruptcies listed on his public records that could be bringing down his scores.

☐He has 3 good paying accounts that have balances near or atthe top of his credit limit. He could pay those down and increase his scores very easily

☐He has $ 400 in collections that are all medical and fairly new so he needs to dispute those so he can possibly remove them.

As you can see I work with all types of credit to make dreams of home ownership a reality.

Now let's look at our final Credit Report and attempt to repair it.

This credit report is different from the credit reports above because this one has recent late payments and all derogatory accounts.

In fact this person's home is in trouble. She came to me to see if there was a way to refinance her home. She was honest and told me that she was late on her mortgage payments and other bills also.

As a loan officer I have the responsibility to everyone to do what I can to help them out financially. This woman was desperate for help and her credit report shows it.

Credit Report- Credit Repair Analysis #3

This is another Credit Report that needs credit repair for us to study.

1 is the date of the credit report. The date is 2/26/2013.

#2 is the middle credit score. TransUnion is the middle repository with a 552 middle score.

#3 is Public Records that records a 9 year old bankruptcy. Only one more year and this can be removed permanently.

#4 is the mortgage history; this mortgage is 60 days late and has a past due balance of $4239 in payments and a balance of $96891

As you can see this mortgage is in trouble. Now before we can go any further, this mortgage history automatically disqualifies the borrower for a FHA mortgage until 12 months of 0 late payments have been recorded.

It is very hard to completely remove active late mortgage payments. The best credit repair services cannot remove something that is totally true and reporting accurately.

But, it can still be worth a try to contact a debt consolidation service to see if an agreement can be reached on the past due amount.

Notice on the next credit report page is the non-derogatory accounts. As you can see this borrower has no good paying account. In other words every account has been late or charged-off.

Next are the derogatory accounts

#1 is Barclay Bank and it is a closed account that was 120 days late

#2 is Fed Loan Service that once was 150 days late but is current now.

#3 and #4 are both collection accounts that are only 2 years old. There are 4 more pages of collections, charged-off accounts and accounts with late payments.

How do you repair a credit account like this? How do you raise credit scores with a credit bureau like this one?

My first suggestion is to add more positive credit accounts. I would do a credit enhancement or add some secured credit cards to give the credit scoring system something to work with.

In order to have a positive credit report you must sustain positive credit and trade-lines to add positive points to a credit bureau.

Where can this person go with a credit report like this?

It is the mortgage that this client was primarily concerned with. She wanted to refinance her mortgage and save her home.

In this case, the best option for her maybe a chapter 13 bankruptcy.

Under bankruptcy laws, the courts can stop any proceeding and arrange a payment plan that can meet the buyer's finances. This can be a life line to rescue her home and her financials.

Once her bankruptcy is over 2 years this credit report can be repaired and she can possibly qualify for a FHA mortgage.

There you have it.

We took 3 credit bureaus and diagnosed them to see how to repair and restore their credit. This book is not the end all for credit repair, but a start to teach what is on the credit reports and how to read a credit report.

With the proper understanding of how credit bureaus work good credit can be achieved and maintained despite your bad experiences in the past.

I began this book telling a story about Billy Walters the professional gambler that I knew in the past.

Billy Walters was not born with a silver spoon in his mouth. He was actually born rather poor and on the wrong side of the financial tracks of life.

But, Billy Walters made his fortune selling used cars. His reputation was that he was the hardest working car salesman in town. Rumor has it that he sold more cars in a 24 hour period than anyone in the country. Billy Walters worked hard to get where he is today.

In order to clean up a credit report and develop an A+ credit rating it takes hard work and dedication.

If you can work hard to repair your credit report and then develop a Billy Walters mindset and treat their credit like he treats his word you could graduate into the high credit score segment of our society.

You can eventually develop a 700 plus credit score like some of my old clients and become credit worthy everywhere you go.

Chapter 4: How Student Loans Default Affect You?

If handle wisely student loans can help you build an excellent credit score. I personally was able to buy my first home at the age of 23 years old because my timely payments on my student loans created for me a great credit history. However, at such a young age, I was not aware of the consequence if I didn't pay my loan on time or defaulted on my student loans. I was blessed to be hired at in 1998 Ford Motor Company while I was attending school. Ford Motor Company has an excellent salary and that help me to repay my loans on time. I spoke on this in my book" **A quick guide on how to boost your credit fast with merchandise cards**", on how student loan debt affects your credit score debt to income ratio.

Unfortunately with the today's economy, the jobs are not available for college graduates as they were in the 90's and many young Americans are defaulting on their student loans.

Student Loans Affects On Credit.

Student loans on your report will help you quickly get a good FICO score as long as you make the payments on time but if you default on your loan it can devastate your credit for years to come. Plus, deferral and forbearance options make it possible to postpone repaying your student loans without lowering your credit score.

Late student loan payments and defaults have an immediate negative effect on your credit report. A late payment of more than 30 days will begin to impact your credit score by 30 points or more and the longer your student loan payments are late, the lower your credit score will drop.

When the lender concludes that you will never pay your student loan, and report that you have defaulted on the student loan. The both default and late payments are now reported on your credit by the lender. Unlike normally debts at only stay on your report for 7 years; student loan will remain on your credit history forever until you pay the loan back in full.

Federal loans allow the debtor to defer or forebear payments; major of private loans doesn't offer this option. This doesn't affect your score, but it can influence a lender's decision on whether to approve you for a loan in the future.

A loan deferral is a temporary period during which time you do not have to pay the principal balance of your loan. For example, if you have a $10,000 student loan in deferral, you do not have to pay any of the loans back at that time period. You may, however, still have to pay interest that accrues on the student loan while in deferral. If the loan carries 5% interest, you may still have to pay for this interest, in this example, about $41.67 per month.

However, forbearances are granted and reviewed on a case-by-case basis, and allow people to postpone repaying their student loans for a fixed period of time.

These two options don't show up on your credit report so deferrals and forbearances have the same impact on your credit, it will appear as "current" on your credit report and impacts your credit score just as if you had been making payments on time.

Student loans also affected your debt-to-income ratio. In my book A quick guide on how to boost your credit fast with merchandise cards, I speak about how my student loans and my mortgage began to lower my credit score because the debts caused me to have a high debt-to-income ratio. All my loans was paid on time but the high debt amount made me look as a high risk to the lenders. I used a technique using merchandise cards to help boost my low credit score.

A borrows' student loan monthly payments is factored into your debt-to-income ratio. Lenders look at this debt when they consider extended mortgages, car loans, personal loans, and business loans. Student loans can make it harder for you to obtain other loans until they are paid completely off.

There are some rare cases in which student loans are cancelled or forgiven, usually as abonus for people who sign up for volunteer or military service, or for others in specific occupations with loan forgiveness programs that we will discuss later on in this chapter. In some extreme situations of financial hardship, loan forgiveness may be available.To the Credit bureaus' student loan cancellation and forgiveness all looks the same: It's a debt discharge caused by non-credit factors, and loan forgiveness does not have any impact on your credit score. Some lenders may inquire why the loans were cancelled before granting a mortgage or personal loan.

In summary the only way to lessen student loans affect on credit is to find away to remove your loans from default and payoff the student loans. We will speak on options to help you to began to start the process of repaying your student loans and programs for loan forgiveness that you may qualify for to eliminate your student loans.

Chapter 5: Your Credit Report

Want to know what the first step is? It is simple, find out where you stand now. I have counselled a lot of people with bad credit – I even used to have bad credit myself so I know how scary this step can be.

After all, it is one thing to know at the back of your mind that you have a bad credit score but it is quite another to actually confront that score in black and white on the page. This is scary – it basically means that you can no longer deny how bad things actually are.

If, however, you can bring yourself to do it anyway, you are actually freeing yourself from a lot of worries in the future – you might even find out that things are not as bad as you thought. You really do not have much of a choice – you need to see your report to see how to go about fixing it.

Getting Your Credit Report

It is not that hard to lay hands on your credit report – in fact, you simply have to apply to the credit bureaus – you are entitled to one free credit report annually.

It is important to apply for your report from each of the three major credit bureaus – Experian, Transunion, and Equifax as the reports can vary from one to the next. Basically, it depends on which unions your credit providers subscribe to. (The credit bureaus basically just amalgamate the information received from the various credit providers in order to generate your payment profile and FICO score.)

If you do not want to apply to each individual site, there are websites that will do this for you – all you will need to do is to provide the relevant information and they will submit the requests to the credit bureaus on your behalf.

Now Let's Look at That Report

Now that you have your report in front of you, you need to start looking at it objectively – pretend that it is a stranger's report and that they have asked you to lend them money. You need to look at the report as if you were the lender, not the borrower and there will be a few things that you need to consider. Let's go through these individually.

What Type of Credit do you Have?

Credit is credit, right? Well, and I have to admit that this was something that surprised me when I learned about it, no – the type of credit that you utilize is used as an indicator of whether you are a responsible lender or not.

Now, in general, credit can be divided up into two broad categories – revolving credit and installment credit. Revolving credit, like the kind that you get with a credit card, is a more open-ended arrangement – as long as you are managing it properly and are paying as you should, you will still have access to the full credit limit. In essence, this means that you could use all the funds, less fees, and interest, that you pay into the card. You could, potentially, never pay off this debt.

An installment credit agreement is not open-ended at all. You will choose the term that you wish to repay your debt at and you will need to make those monthly payments as agreed. As the term of the loan progresses, the balance of the debt is reduced and, normally, you will not be allowed to draw that money out again.

Which do you think is considered riskier when it comes to new potential lenders?

Your Payment History

You remember when you thought that you could just slide on the last month's payment, or you just missed it by a couple of days? All that information is recorded on your payment history. And, even if you pay your accounts as little as one day late every month, you will be listed as a slow payer.

This is something that people just don't often realize – the importance of paying your bills on time every month. Your payment history is one of the things that a potential creditor will look at carefully because past behavior is the best predictor of future behavior. If you have a long string of late payments, that gives the impression that you are unable to afford your current debt or that you are irresponsible when it comes to paying bills – either way, it is a bad reflection on you as a borrower.

And it is good to remember that whilst the FICO score only takes the latest 6 months into account, your full payment history for each account is still listed. So that means that you need to be consistent in your efforts and keep up the new good behavior as anyone viewing your credit report will be able to see the full payment history.

How Much Debt You Might Get Into

This is another thing that people seldom realize makes a difference. Let us say that you are a responsible borrower and never max out your cards – what are your credit limits? A potential creditor will need to look at the overall amount of debt that you might be able to access – maybe today you haven't used your store card limit but there is nothing stopping you from doing so at a later stage.

If you went and spent just an extra $500 on 4 of your cards, your debt could, for example, have increased by $2000 in an instant and your whole repayment profile would have changed as well.

How Many Accounts You Have

The fact is that credit is a fickle mistress – you have to have some accounts that you pay in order to prove that you are credit worthy. Once you have proved that you are credit worthy, it will seem as though everyone wants to offer you credit. The problem with having too many credit accounts from a creditor's point of view is not only that you have a higher potential exposure.

It can also be viewed as a sign that you are unable to manage your finances. Why do you have 3 credit cards and 5 store cards, if you are so good at managing your money?

How Much do you Actually Owe?

This is a big one, obviously but there are a couple of different things to consider under this heading.

First of all, how much is your overall exposure to debt and how does this affect your ability to repay it? Creditors want to see that you can not only manage the debt that you currently have but also that you can manage the debt that you are applying for.

Repayments for debt, excluding mortgage debt, should be, at most, 30% of your overall monthly salary – AFTER deductions. Your mortgage should not exceed 30% of your overall monthly salary AFTER deductions either.

More importantly for creditors, though, is how you utilize the credit that you do already have. It is in this area that most people actually come short when it comes to the difference between that great credit score and the good or fair one.

Think about it for a second, if your friend had maxed out all their cards and gotten loans all over the place and then still came over to you to come and get a loan, would you be happy to give it to them?

Constantly maxing out your credit limits, especially when these are revolving credit limits, is a strong indicator of one of two things – either you have more debt than you can handle and need to use credit to supplement your income or you are irresponsible when it comes to spending. If you want to fall into the excellent category

in terms of your FICO score, you should
not be using over 30% of your credit limits
at any stage. (does not apply to mortgage
limits)

Chapter 6: Fixing Bad Credit With Good Credit

If you're looking to improve your credit score there are a few things you want to do. The first is to get your current credit under control so you can turn it into good credit. The other is to get additional good credit. Now if you still have credit cards and they have not been taken that's great. Even if you have an outstanding debt on those cards they can be used in your favor. Make sure that you're not losing the cards.

Now, if you have an outstanding balance on your cards take a moment to write it down. List each card that currently has a balance, how much the balance is and how much is late. This may seem depressing when you look at the amount of debt that you have but it's important to understand. Some of the smaller debts may be possible to get rid of quickly if you're careful and you think it through. Some of the larger ones you may be able to work with pretty well at the same time.

Consider what your income is and what money you have available to spend towards your debts. Do you have enough that you could pay off a few of the smaller debts and still leave a couple credit cards open? If you do that's great. What you want to do is call up the company and negotiate with them. Offer them a smaller amount than what is owed and tell them that if they are willing to accept that amount you can pay them immediately. Most credit card companies will jump at the offer. Even if you offer them $100 or more less than what is actually owed they will be perfectly happy taking the money because they know it's at least going to get them something. On the other hand if they refuse there's no telling if you'll declare bankruptcy and then they will never get their money.

Paying off the cards will effectively close them because your credit granting company is going to take the card away from you as soon as they get their money. That's why you don't actually want to pay off all the cards that you have debt with. If you pay them all off then you're going to lose every one of them and that's going to result in no new credit being added to your credit report. That's actually going to hurt you even more than it's going to help. It may seem strange since you're looking at debt (which hurts your credit) but if you close out those accounts it's actually going to be worse than if you keep that debt hanging around at least a little while longer.

What you need to do is start making payments. Even if you owe a lot of money to a credit card company or a loan company they will rarely close the account or turn it over to a collections agency if you are making payments. They'll wait until you stop paying because, at the moment at least, they can expect to get their full amount back. If they sell the account to a collections agency they will get only a small percentage of the actual amount owed from the company. By making payments on time you increase your credit score because the algorithm that's used to calculate on time payments doesn't consider whether the actual amount due is past due. All it focuses on is whether the payment is made by the due date.

When you continue making those on time payments you also have credit. If you have credit this also counts in your favor. If you close those accounts you lose the open credit that you have and your credit score will actually go down (even though you've gotten rid of debt). So make sure you keep those cards open and don't completely pay off the amount that's owed. Once you get the balance to a level that you can manage continue to make additional purchases and pay them. This is going to build your good credit even faster.

Once you've managed to pay the outstanding debt your credit company is less likely to pull your card away as quickly because you will still have new charges to pay off and they now have a little more trust that you're going to pay it back to them. They will likely allow you to keep the card and that's going to increase your ability to build credit. Having the open credit and then having a low minimum balance on the cards will increase your score by a lot.

What a low balance means is that you make sure not to spend a lot of money on your credit cards and you keep the balance low. When you open credit cards you are given a limit. That's the amount of money that you are allowed to spend on that card. When you keep the balance (the amount you have spent) at the low end of this limit it actually improves your credit score. When it's high your credit score tends to go down. But you don't have to be careful about each credit card (though that's the best way to do it).

All of your credit cards are added together in order to create your total balance. So if you have three credit cards for $1,000, $1,500 and $500 your total available credit is $3,000. If your $500 credit card is completely maxed out but you haven't spent anything on the others then your credit score is still going to be pretty good because your total balance is about 16% of your available credit. On the other hand if you had maxed out the most expensive card your credit used would be about 50%

and this is not going to look so good on your credit score.

In order to improve your bad credit it's important to pay attention to your balances. Try to keep them down and try to make payments on them frequently. This is going to help you develop a track record for trustworthiness and that's going to ensure that other credit companies are willing to give you credit and willing to let you keep that credit as well. If at all possible you want to make sure that this happens because the only way to build your credit is through having credit. Just getting rid of the debt isn't going to do enough.

Another thing to keep in mind is that you want to work with the credit card companies and loan companies. If at all possible do not let your accounts go to a collection agency. You will pay a lot more money to a collection agency and it's also going to look even worse on your credit report. Plus it's going to stay on your credit report a lot longer than the late payments to your credit card company. Even if you have to make a lot of payments over a long span of time you'll be better off this way.

Finally, if you don't have credit cards open right now you want to get them. You want to have at least three cards that have revolving credit. That means you want three credit cards that you are using and making timely payments on. If you do this it's going to help you improve your score even as you work towards fixing some of your other problems.These new cards may have to be secured because the company does not trust your credit score and believes you will default on the money that may or may not be owed to them.

Make sure that you get the credit. Take small credit cards with secured amounts and make sure that you pay them on time. If you do this it's going to boost your score. You will definitely be surprised how quickly those positive ratings will start to show up as well. Just take advantage of them and keep building your credit. We'll explain a little more on how to get rid of some of the negative accounts in the next few chapters and how to keep your credit going strong once you've managed to fix it.

Chapter 7: What's Your Fico Score

You have heard it again and again, your FICO score must be so high to get this type of credit, this kind of interest rate, and this type of privilege. The FICO score is the single most important factor that stands between you and just about anything you want to get.

While many people fully understand the impact of the FICO score on their credit, few people, if asked, could actually tell you what it is or how it is determined. Given the weight that this number holds over so many people, it seems amazing that more people don't ask what it is or what they can do about it. They just simply accept the fact that this number has so much power in their lives.

Most people do not realize that the credit bureau that issues your reports does not determine your score, it is done by another company, a third party called the

Fair, Isaac Corporation (FICO). They weigh all the different elements of your credit report to determine what number you get. All the data collected by the credit bureaus are factored in to come up with a three-digit number.

This is probably the only grade you should seriously worry about after you get out of school. It is the grade you get for your financial stability. That single three-digit number will tell the world what they should think about you. But it is not a number that reflects only the present it is also a pathway to your future as well. If anything is wrong with your reports, it is your responsibility to get it fixed. This is the primary and most effective way to change it.

For this reason, it is important that you know what's in your report so that you can correct any information that is incorrect or incomplete. This will help to bring your score up higher. Very few people have a perfect score of 950, but you can improve that number if you know what to do.

How are the Numbers Determined

When your FICO score is determined, several factors must be taken into consideration. The actual score is calculated based on their order of importance.

35% is based on your payment history. As long as you pay your bills on time, this part of your score will be high.

30% is based on how much money you owe. It is called your credit utilization ratio. While you want to be using your credit, you don't want to be using 100% of it. When you are maxed out credit wise, it can have an impact on how high your score will be. Try to aim to spend no more than 30% of your total credit limit to get an optimal balance.

15% is based on your credit history. The longer you have had credit, the better.

10% is based on the different types of credit you have. A nice combination is always good to see. If you have credit card debt, a mortgage, and installment loans, it shows that you are versatile when it comes to credit and you can handle all sorts of things responsibility.

10% is based on new credit. You don't want to go out and apply for a bunch of loans to get new credit, but if you have some new credit, it looks very positive and could have a positive effect on your score.

Having information like this can go a long way in helping you to see what kind of things actually are involved in determining your credit score. As you can see, all of it is important but being able to see exactly where your weak points are can give you a specific target area you can focus on improving.

No one knows the exact formula for calculating a credit score. The Fair Isaacs Corporation is pretty tight-lipped when asked about the specific algorithms they use. However, as you can see from the above, much of the weight is based on your payment history. That's why it is so important that you find a way to pay your bills as soon as they come due. By doing this, you can be sure that you'll have a leg up when it comes to repairing your credit.

You Have More Than One Credit Score

There is no doubt that the FICO score is the number one score merchants refer to when deciding whether or not to issue you credit but it is not the only one. There are other scores that potential creditors may also choose to refer to. For example, Vantage Score, a system developed by the credit bureaus themselves, will also have a number for you. In fact, many agencies give merchants your credit score.

When you apply for credit, you never know which score the merchant will refer to, so it is very important that you do everything you can to improve your credit from every aspect. While there may not be a huge difference between them, you can never be too cautious. The good news is that every credit score, regardless of which agency determines, will be based on the same information, the credit reports you have with the agencies.

How to Check Your Credit Score

One of the first things you need to do is to check what your score actually is. This will give you a starting point to work with and help you to lay out a plan of action. If you know you have had some troubled spots in your history, the best time to check it is now, before you apply for any new credit.

While there are many ways you can get your credit score, the primary source is through one of the three main credit bureaus, Experian, Equifax, and TransUnion. These reporting houses are the go-to places for most potential creditors considering. Because of this, you really want to know what information they have collected from you so you can verify its accuracy.

Many people do not realize this, but it is a federal law that allows you to view your credit reports at least once a year. It might seem strange, but there was a time when you would not have been allowed to see what information had been collected about you. The credit bureaus felt that since you would not have been their

78

primary consumer, they were not obligated to inform you about any information collected concerning you. However, a federal law issued about 25 years ago changed all of that. Now, you can check your report from each of these agencies at least once a year.

If you have not checked your report in a long time, it is strongly advised that you check all three. If you have checked it, then it is recommended that you pull from one agency once every four months so that you can see exactly what has changed on your report and make corrections as soon as they happen. Getting a copy is pretty easy. First, go to AnnualCreditReport.com and follow the instructions for requesting your report.

Scan

Once you have your report in your hand, the first thing you want to do is scan for any information that may be incorrect. It could be something as simple as a wrong address or something as major as bankruptcy or a collection debt that has been paid off. Your first objective is to identify any errors and take the steps to fix them immediately. Just this simple tactic can boost your credit score immeasurably.

In some rare instances, there may not be enough of a credit history to justify getting a score. Even in such situations, it is important that you know this and work to establish credit so that you have something for the merchant to analyze.

Chapter 8: How To Save For An Emergency Fund Effectively

Most financial crises come about as a result of not having savings, or enough savings, put aside in the event that something unexpected should happen. One of the most important aspects of credit repair is to take sensible steps to improve your credit score and try to prevent another financial disaster from ever happening again. It is hard work to get back on track and build up your credit score. The last thing you want is for disaster to strike again. One of the ways to prevent this is to have an emergency fund for your household. Most experts recommend that an emergency fund should contain at least three to six months' worth of living expenses. You also need to calculate that if you were to lose your job, it might take you as long as six months to find a new one, especially if you were earning at a high level or there are many people in your field. Unemployment or illness can take their toll on your finances.

If you have not been saving regularly up until now, it can be hard to develop the habit of saving; however, as we have said, we are sure you can find some areas of your budget that can be tightened, and the short-term sacrifices that you make for the next few weeks and months can lead to long-term security.

Your primary objective will be to pay down debt in order to improve your credit score because the interest rates you are paying on your credit card balances are far higher than anything that you can expect to earn from a savings account, money market account, or other liquid investment, that is, an investment from which you can easily access the money should you ever need to.

Having said that, do be sure to leave yourself a cushion just in case so that you are not tempted to use your credit cards, and open bank accounts for any projected expenses you know are coming up. For example, a Christmas club is a traditional way to spread out the cost of the holidays, gifts, food and entertainment, and travel, over a period of several months. Thanks to the wonders of modern technology, you can get a reminder email telling you when the next payment needs to be made or the payment can be deducted from your checking account automatically.

Other items might be for vacation to visit family, or unusual day care expenses in the summer when the children are out of school, especially if both of you are working and do not get very much vacation time.

Jim has written an entire guide on how to build an emergency fund for step by step instructions. For now, it is enough to say that you should put aside some savings every month to act as a cushion against the unexpected.

It does not make sense to put a lot of money in a savings account at this point, however, if you are paying a lot of interest on your credit card balances. You can put a small amount aside each month, but otherwise, make the rest of your money go to work for you by paying down your debt.

When you are about 50 to 75 percent of the way through paying down your credit card balances and you have been snowballing your payments from your previous cards, you can start diverting some of the money you have been using to paying down your debt as rapidly possible.

Then it will make sense to start building your emergency fund. Once all the credit cards are paid off, you can then fill your emergency fund with six months of living expenses based on your current budget. Don't go wild and start feeling as if you can relax financially. Stick to your goals of getting out of debt, staying out of debt and creating a more secure financial future.

Keep saving in the emergency fund and any other savings accounts for things that are important to you and your family.

Remember, you are not supposed to use credit cards again unless there is a good reason to do so, such as cash back or money in a 529 account. Be sure to limit your spending to keep with your new good habits and not spend every penny of your paycheck.

One of the best ways to do this is to not take any bill for granted. Look at your utility bills, cable, mobile phones and more to find the best deals. It's your money. Make every penny count, and make the money you save go to work for you by paying down your debt and boosting your credit score. Once you have accomplished this, you can then start to think not only about saving, but investing wisely as well.

Another area you should look at in relation to emergencies is whether or not you have enough insurance, and the right kinds of insurance. Jim deals with life insurance in his beginner's guide on the subject, and there are a range of other insurance options to help cushion the blow of unexpected events. Insurance can help protect you in case of emergencies, to keep costs manageable. Even pet insurance is essential these days, with the average pet emergency treatment at the veterinarian costing over $3,000. As we have said, budgeting, saving and managing your money by reviewing your finances regularly and paying down your debt strategically will all help improve your credit score. Protecting what you have and saving for emergencies, plus being proactive before any emergency ever happens again, can help protect you from the kinds of financial disasters which probably caused you to get into financial difficulties in the first place. When we discuss budgets with people, we always point out that they are meant to be flexible enough to allow for some wiggle room, not a strait jacket, but also not so flexible that you start having money problems again. One of the areas that people overlook most in their budget is the line or lines relating to their income.

Action **Steps**

1-Open a new bank account for savings at a bank or a credit union. Try to get one with interest, or one with no fees. Use this account as your emergency fund and do not touch it unless there is a real financial crisis.

2-Open additional accounts if they do not carry fees to help save for your other financial goals. Open a 529 account if available in your state and you wish to save for college for any children you may have.Set up a Christmas club account if you have a lot of end of year holiday commitments you wish to budget for across all 12 months of the year rather than just one.

3-Make a list of all of your savings goals, starting with short-term goals, then mid- to long-term goals.If you can, place a dollar value next to each goal. Write down any date by which you wish to accomplish the goal, such as the date your first child should be heading off to college. Check the balances on the accounts you set up in Step 2 regularly to see if you are on target with your goals.

Thus far in this guide we have been discussing getting out of financial difficulties with your current level of income, with things as they are at the moment, assuming no change other than trying to be more frugal in order to pay down debts more quickly. But what if you could institute another small change or two, however, with you and your spouse, and perhaps even the children taking on some work, to bring more income into your household? Working a second job or even starting your own small business can also help bring in more money to pay down your debts and rescue your credit score even more rapidly. Let's look at this topic in the next chapter.

Chapter 9: Improving Your Score—The Right Way 5

There might be different factors for your failure to repay a loan on time. Whatever be the reason, if someone has not repaid a loan on time, it will surely affect his credit record and his rating will come down significantly. With the lowering of credit rating, the chances for getting a loan in future will also be reduced. Therefore, you should always try to pay back your loan on time and keep your credit record unaffected. However, if you have already got a poor record, you should learn how to improve credit score.

If you want to get your record repaired, you need to be careful about the expenses you are making. Be more calculative about the money that you are spending and try to save as much as possible. Use the saved money in repaying the old debts and getting your score repaired. When you have a huge amount of outstanding, you should know how to improve credit score fast by manipulating your money.

Someone who is worried about his low score and wants to know how to improve the score easily should stop the use of credit cards at once. In most of the cases, people incur huge debts after credit card shopping. So, it is always advisable to stop using such cards when you want to get your ratings repaired. Even if you use a card, you should make sure to do proper calculations before making any transaction with it.

Student's credit cards are one of the most prominent causes of getting bad credits. If this is the same in your case and you want to know how to improve your score quickly, you should get the student card of your child blocked immediately. Whether someone has the bad record or not, it is never advisable to allow your child use a card as he/she does not have any idea regarding the right use of this card.

When you want to know how to improve your score, you can always take the assistance of financial experts, who can offer proper consultation against some charges. Debt settlement and debt consolidation are some of the most important ways of getting your score improved. By taking these services, you can get your loan repaid in a few installments. Yet, before taking any of these services, you should always spend some time to note the pros and cons of each of the services.

If like many of us, your credit score is less than perfect, there are several ways you can improve it. Now you could hire a credit repair company to help you with this, but I suggest you save your money. Realistically, there is not much they can do for you that you can't do for yourself if you just know how. Sure, they'll charge you lots of money and 2 years and $2000 later your score won't look any better than if you had saved yourself the $2000 and done the work yourself.

Improve your payment history

Start making our payments on time and avoid late payments at all costs.

Clear up past bills quickly paying off high-interest bills first. This saves you money in interest fees and reduces your total debt and time needed to pay off debts.

Contact your creditors to see if a lower, more manageable payment can be arranged.

Ask if charge-offs can be removed from your record and accounts reopened.

See if creditors will erase late payment entries when you start paying on time.

Decrease outstanding debts

Pay debts that have higher interest rates first.

Keep balances low and keep revolving debt such as credit cards to 30% of available credit.

Never close old unused accounts quickly. This can have a negative effect on your score.

Close accounts slowly and check your credit report to be sure the closed accounts are listed as closed by consumer.

Get a better history

If your credit history is new, do not open a lot of accounts quickly. Creditors perceive this as a sign that you can not manage your credit.

Manage credit effectively

Don't open a new account with a large credit limit but rather confine your account at a medium limit.

Do not open too many accounts at once.

Consider credit payments when making your budget.

Do not apply for too many accounts at once since these inquiries can negatively affect your score.

Keep a proper mix of the right results

Too many installment loans reduce your score since the payments remain the same over time.

A combo of credit cards and installment loans is it ideal mix. However, manage the cards effectively, staying within the 30% of available credit range. Pay these balances quickly.

Open a savings account. This action will encourage your creditors to think you are saving money to pay down your debts.

Finally, remember to make your payments on time and monitor your credit report. Remove any errors from this report.

Chapter 10: Enroll In Automatic Bill Pay

"Since signing up for automatic bill pay, I have much more relaxed and carefree. I no longer have to worry about paying all 17 of my credit card bills or forgetting to pay a few of them altogether."

One important thing you must do is to pay your bills on time. This has one of the biggest, if not the biggest, impacts on your credit score. One way to make sure you are paying all of your bills on time is by setting up an automatic payment plan. This can easily be set up through your bank or credit union. If you one time payments on an account for at least 6 months, you can increase your credit score by as much as 50 points according to experts.

You can lessen your credit card payoff time from making minimum payments that will take 12-14 years to payoff, to 4 to 5 years, by setting up automatic bill pay and continuing to pay the same amount even after your minimum payment has been lowered by your creditors. Do this each and every month, and you will pay off your Credit Card in 4 to 5 years instead of 12-14 years. So, for example, if you pay a $40 per month minimum, keep paying $40 every month; do not lower your monthly payment by the $4 or $5 that your minimum monthly payment typically drops by. The credit card companies count on you to make the reducing minimum monthly payments (i.e. $40 this month, $36 next month, $35, and so on and so forth), and this is what drags your payoff out 12 to 14 years. So continue paying $40 every month with automated bill pay, even after your minimum payment changes, and watch the pay off drop from 14 to 5 years.

Increase Your Credit Limits

"Hello, are you there? Yeah this is Barack. Listen, I need that increase ASAP."

Ok in all seriousness, if you have been making payments on time and make enough money to sustain a higher credit limit, call your credit card company and ask them to raise your limit. Experts say that a higher credit limit will lower your credit utilization ratio. However, you must also be honest with yourself about knowing whether or not a higher credit limit would tempt you to bury yourself deeper into debt. You do not want to ask for a higher credit limit if you know that deep down there is some particular item that you have your eye on or know that you will be all the more tempted to spend even a little bit of the increase when your goal is to rid yourself of debt and bring that score up. This is an advanced step for those who really believe that they have the discipline to refrain from more unnecessary spending. Remember, most people tend to spend more money when they get more money, but I like to think outside of the poor way of thinking and adapt the habits of the highly successful people out there and I wish the same for you.

It's about knowing yourself, and asking, 'Am I going to be responsible using that credit card?' If your limit is $3,000 and it gets raised to $6,000, and all you end up with is more credit card debt, then you have only added to the problem you were originally trying to remedy. But, for those who can handle it, yes, call and try to get your limit raised so that you are at one third of your credit utilization ratio and thus improving your credit score. But I must repeat, this step is for those with the discipline to handle having more credit. I thought I was one of these disciplined people at one point but I learned the hard way so I am over- stressing this to prevent you from going down the same road.

Random Tip:

Do not apply for store credit cards, even if the initial savings seem tempting. FICO considers people who have store credit cards more of a risk and their credit score calculation algorithm takes this into account, according to former FICO executive Andy Jolls.

Chapter 11: Credit Repair

Credit repair is fairly straightforward to understand. As the name states, it is the process of repairing bad credit history. It can be as simple as fixing some misunderstandings or mistakes with your credit companies. It can also lead to the fixing of your own fundamental financial issues which includes budgeting and addressing the immediate concerns of the lenders. Of course, you cannot simply repair credit like you are fixing your broken wardrobe. It takes a lot of time and patience to repair credit.

It is probably good to note that everything a credit repairing agency can do for you, you can do for yourself at little or no cost! We will go through this in a minute. You have to understand that there is no way for you to wipe off or remove accurate, negative notes (those mentioned in the previous chapter) from your credit report. However, the law allows you to request an investigation of the alleged inaccurate information through a dispute process. If a credit agency cannot verify certain negative information on your credit report, they are obliged to remove it.

Without further ado, here are some easy steps you can take to repair your credit! (Reminder: To achieve this, you must have patience and persistence. Credit agencies are not the most cooperative or efficient people around).

1) Obtain Your Credit Report – For more details on this step, refer to the chapter above. You may request your credit report from all three credit reporting agencies – Equifax, Experian and TransUnion.

2) Analyze Credit Report – This is the next logical step to take! After you have obtained your credit report, carefully scrutinize it to extract the blemishes in the report so that you can tackle them one by one. For more information on what to look out for, refer to Chapter 2.

3) Prioritize Your Target – Once you have scrutinized your report, you want to make a list of all the negative information and rank them in descending order of priority. Priority in this case can mean the amount of damage it is doing to the image of your credit report. As a rule of thumb, you want to remove the most damaging reports first. This will provide you with a focused, concise plan on how to fix your credit history.

4) The Dispute – When you challenge a record, it is very important to go in with the intent to remove the ENTIRE record. For example, if you want to challenge a loan default, you want to prove to the credit agency that the loan doesn't exist at all so they will remove the entire note from your report. You don't want to dispute the number of days you delayed the payments for – yes, you delayed for 35 days instead of 55 days, but the truth is that your negative record remains in the report.

Generally, you want to dispute everything on your report that is not up to date (personal details, past addresses…). The reason is because identity theft is such a common issue now that you don't want to leave room for the possibility of mix-ups with another person. By removing non-current entries, your agencies may not be able to verify certain information against that old address and this may earn you instant deletion of negative records.

When filing disputes, you want to write to each of the agencies separately. The reason is because your credit reports may differ between these 3 agencies. Additionally, you want to specifically ensure that all 3 agencies update your credit report correctly.

In the dispute letter, you need not produce fancy or technical terms. Be clear and concise on what you are disputing and the reason for it. Here is a brief checklist of things to note and include in the letter – reason for dispute; desired outcome of dispute; be sincere; be rational, not emotional; documentations to substantiate the dispute.

It is very likely that your listings will be concluded as verified. If so, do not give up. You have to change the reasons you provide for the agencies so they have something fresh to look into. A sample of the order of reasons can look like this:

- Not your account

- Wrong amount stated

- Wrong account number

- Erroneous creditors

- Wrong date

- Wrong credit limit

- Wrong status

Switch your reasons each time you challenge a listing in the order of priority listed above.

5) Documentation is Important – So you have ordered your credit reports and created a plan to execute your disputes, the next important thing you have to do now is to create a file or system to track your dispute process in detail.

This can include the email exchanges between the agencies and yourself, photocopies of the letters and documentations, notes on phone conversations (name of person you spoke to, as well as the time and the date). Now you might be asking – why go to this extent of trouble? Well, the reason is because certain listings that have been removed because of your hard work can re-appear with no apparent reason!

Sounds ridiculous? Absolutely – but it has happened before. Fortunately, as long as you are able to provide documented proof of what has been previously agreed upon that led to the original deletion of the entry, it is not difficult to remove it the second time.

6) The Waiting Game – Once your dispute has been received, the investigations will begin. The law states that credit reporting agencies must resolve consumer disputes within 30 days. You will receive written notice of the results of their investigation within 3 to 5 days of its completion. However, it is often noted that because of the high volume of consumer complaints on inaccurate credit report, the problem may take up to 6 months to be resolved.

7) Evaluating Results – After you have received your report back from your agency, you will find that your items will most likely have been resolved in one of the three ways:

1) Listing is not mentioned – This means that your issue has not been resolved accurately. You need to check your dispute claim to see if you have included it. You probably need to dispute it again in the next letter.

2) Investigated but verified – This means that your listing is not removed and the reason provided is that it is verified. You may choose to re-submit a fresh dispute to prove that the item is incorrect or invalid. If you missed out on sending any documentation, now is the time to provide it.

3) Unverifiable – This means that the item in contention is found to be inaccurate or unverifiable. In this case, the item should be removed from the report altogether!

One critical thing to ensure is that the positive entries are not being removed. Credit agencies are notorious for disputing all items and routinely remove positive entries.

8) Request Method of Verification – Do not settle just because a dispute came back as verified. Instead, it is your right to request for the method of verification and the credit agency has to provide this information to you within 15 days of this request. This is a great way to force agencies into re-evaluating their investigations.

9) Request for Proof from Creditors – The creditors have to be able to provide proof to the negative listing in your credit report. As such, you want to write in to the creditors and ask for such proof. In the event that they are unable to do so, they will be in violation of the Fair Credit Reporting Act (FCRA) and have to remove it from your credit report.

10) Rinse and Repeat! – Repeat the above steps for all your negative listings and across all 3 credit agencies. As we have mentioned before, credit repairing process takes time and cannot be rushed. You have to be more and more persistent with each dispute. Know your rights and play by the law. It does not hurt to mention that you will bring in an attorney to settle the case for you. Another tip is not to flood the agencies with your dispute letters. Although they cannot legally stop you from doing so, this will probably overwhelm them and be counterproductive.

Chapter 12: Communicating With Creditors And Bureaus

Negotiate your way to a discounted payoff

Once you take an inventory of your debts owed, you can begin negotiating a discounted payoff beginning with your collection accounts less than two years old. These are the accounts with the greatest negative impact on your credit score. The way debt collection works, your debt is in most cases sold by your original credit to a debt collection agency at a deep discount, and that company is left to recover as much of your outstanding debt as possible.

For example, let's say Company A is a debt collection corporation. They buy all of Store A's bad credit card accounts. Store A has already charged off your outstanding balance on their accounting books as a loss, so they will sell the right to collect the debt to Company A for .05 on the dollar. If you owe Store A $500, Company A will buy they debt for $1. They then have a set period of time to attempt to collect as much of that debt as possible. Economies of scale allow debt collection companies to buy large amounts of bad debt for extremely deep discounts, and that's how they make their profits. By disputing or asking for the debt to be validated by Company A, you can find out how much they paid for the debt which gives you great leverage when negotiating a discounted payoff. Your ability to negotiate a discounted payoff will vary case-by-case. However, whatever you negotiate be sure to request in writing that the debt will be reported, "Paid as Agreed." This way when a potential lender reviews your credit report, he or she will not see a bad debt, they will only see that you "Paid as Agreed." Debt collectors have the ability to report this information to credit bureaus how they please, so do not accept anything less than "Paid as Agreed" when negotiating and get it in writing before making a payment.

Also, never allow a creditor to debit your bank account, unless you set up a separate account to pay off debts. Always mail the payment or pay by some other means that does not include your bank account being debited. This protects you as a consumer from any unwanted payments being made from your account. By law, creditors have to give you more than one payment option. For example, you may settle on $200 for a $500 debt, but the debt collector may accidently debit your account for $500. Not all debt collectors are this vicious, but better safe than sorry. As a rule of thumb, you have already shown a debt collector you will go without paying by having your account in collections. Do not hesitate to walk away from negotiating a payoff if the debt collector does not want to work out a deal favorable to your terms. For a debt less than two years old, I suggest you offer 40-60% of the amount you originally owed. Their job is to collect debt and they earn a handsome commission for doing so. Remember this is business, and no matter how friendly and cordial the conversation, if you do not get what you want from the negotiations, you lost. Debt collectors are not your friend, they are doing their job.

Create and tell your own financial story

Prior to having an account forwarded to collections, if you find yourself on hard times, write an explanation letter detailing your situation to your creditor. Do this before your account is reported 60 or 90 days past due. You might ask for a reduced monthly payment for a set number of months. You may ask for a forbearance period or you may ask that a month's payment be added to the end of your note if it is for an installment account. In business everything is negotiable, so you can ask for what you please, and the creditor may respond accordingly. Just like any other relationship, communication is key.

Creditors are not the only ones who can make statements on your credit report. You can also send a letter to each credit reporting bureau in the form of a consumer statement. This statement might be a brief summary of a financial hardship that causes two accounts to become delinquent. Within reason, you can add any statement to your credit report. This will allow a potential lender better understand why you have accounts reported 30 days late in the past 24 months. Your consumer statement may ultimately help you receive a favorable lending decision if you have corrected much of your negative account information since that time.

In addition to having your consumer statement added to your credit report, you may also consider the fairly new self-reporting strategy. A website and service provider that is increasing in popularity for self-reporting is Pay Rent Build Credit.To get a PRBC Score and Report, become a member and register at least three monthly-billed accounts. These might be your rent, your electric bill, your cable bill or even an online service. Then, all you have to do is be sure to pay your bills on time every month. PRBC might not yet have the clout of the big three credit bureaus, but a solid report from PRBC might be enough to get your foot in the door with a lender.

Every city will have local organizations offering assistance to people seeking credit counseling. If not, there should be one within one hour driving distance. Financial literacy is becoming more and more of a mainstream issue as the millennial generation continues to transition into their strongest income earning years. Be sure to use the resources available to you. Know there is hope and light at the end of the tunnel for you even if you are currently in an unsatisfactory financial situation, no matter your race or national origin. In today's Digital Age, you only need to use your freedom of creativity to realize more opportunities for you and your family. Likewise, by the numbers, Millennials (people born 1980-2000) are the largest generation of consumers on earth currently, and command the most buying power as a result. These are the same people who became adults right around the time of 9/11 and began their professional careers right in line with the Great Recession. As a result, people age 15-35 are experiencing a different economy than generations past. However, the Digital Age offers many more avenues of generating income for those who are creative, ambitious, and committed to earning what many might consider non-conventional income not tied to a 9-5 job. By many accounts, the internet will likely produce more millionaires in this generation than the stock market.

Chapter 13: Where To Get Your Credit Reports

There are three main ways to get your annual credit report (by law, you are allowed to get a copy of your credit report from each of the three main credit bureaus). These agencies don't deal with credit consumers directly. Instead, they have joined hands to have a central place where you can request for a credit report. They have done that through:

*Having a central website where you can request for instant reports at www.annualcreditreport.com

*Having a toll free number where you can call 1-877-322-8228 to request for your free report, which will be mailed within 15 days.

*Having a central mailing address where you can request for your free report through mail by downloading the request form here then mailing it to **Annual Credit**

Report Request Service; the report will be mailed within 15 days. You can actually request for a free annual credit report from each of the biggest credit bureaus at different times or at the same time.

The truth is that a lot happens during the year such that your annual credit report could reflect an already messed up score. You have to track your score every single month if you are serious about repairing your credit. This calls for a credit monitoring service to know what happens during every single month. As you look for a credit monitoring service, insist on finding one that gets you FICO scores and not FAKO scores since these could be different from your FICO score. Most banks and other lending institutions will often use the FICO score so you want to monitor this one. FAKO has been known to give people a false sense of security because it is often higher than the FICO score. You will need to spend money for this one (about $15 per month).

Note:

*Apart from getting your credit score reports from each of the reporting agencies , you may also request for a credit report in cases where you feel you have been unfairly denied credit. You are supposed to notify the agency within 60 days of such an encounter.

*If you have highlighted errors in your regular credit report, and the agencies have confirmed you concerns as merited, you can request for a fresh credit report from them. This report does not count for your regular annual ones you are entitled to. Moreover, you have a right to request the reporting agencies to supply all the organizations that viewed your report in the last six months with the corrected copy each.

Although this might sound like a good idea, remember I mentioned that the credit bureaus have no business in you having a good score so don't be fooled to think that they will do much. There is a lot to learn about your credit report so that you can get off the illusion that things are as rosy as they seem. Every single item in the credit score has a meaning. Some could even be enough grounds for disputing so don't overlook anything. Let me explain how to interpret your credit score in the next chapter.

Chapter 14: Your Credit Report

If you plan to get another credit card, purchase a major asset on mortgage, apply for new utilities connections, or look for a new job, you should know that your credit report can either be your best friend or worst enemy.Why?It's because your credit report, prepared by at least one major credit bureau or agency to whom your creditors send all your credit information, tells financial institutions, your potential employers, and utility companies about your financial risks.Moreover, your financial risks matter in decisions on whether or not to hire you, give you a new line of credit, or give you access to utilities.And considering that credit reports or information therein are crucial for determining your credit score, checking for errors in such and being able to dispute and correct them can help you improve your credit score too.

Check for Possible Errors in Your Reports

Credit reports are prepared by people using information sourced from, well, other people.And because people are humans and no human is perfect, it's certainly possible for your credit reports to contain errors.Such errors can vary in nature and weight, from timely payments that were recorded otherwise to erroneously reported bankruptcy applications that can appear on your credit report and damage your credit score.

Since your credit report can significantly impact some of your most important activities such as job hunting, applying for utilities connections, and borrowing money, you must ensure that your credit reports accurately present who you are financially.Undetected errors run you the risk of a damaged financial reputation.

In countries like the United States, the law guarantees borrowers the right to accurate credit reports.Consequently, credit bureaus are prohibited from filing unsubstantiated, incomplete, and erroneous credit reports.In such countries, the law guarantees borrowers like you the right to contest erroneous facts and figures that appear on your credit report that come from credit bureaus, and demand for their removal from or correction on your credit report.

So how do you check if the credit reports that credit bureaus prepare about you are accurate?The first obvious step is to get your copy of your credit report, which you can do in different ways.One is to obtain a free copy through major credit report websites such as www.AnnualCreditReport.com.Another way is to demand for a free copy of your credit report from credit bureaus, which is your right under the following circumstances in certain jurisdictions such as the United States:

• You're a recipient of government assistance or welfare;

• You're looking for a job and are currently unemployed;

• You've been a recent victim of identity theft; or

• Your recent credit, job or utilities connection application has been turned down because of negative information contained in your credit report and very low credit score.

In some places in the United States, the law entitles you to one free credit report annually.This is on top of the free credit reports you're able to obtain through various other sources.

If a free credit report's not available in your jurisdiction, you can simply buy your copy from the major credit bureaus.For how much?Well, it depends on the credit bureau but typically, credit reports can cost anywhere from $10 to $20 per copy.And when you get reports from different credit bureaus or rating agencies, you must make sure to compare them to each other because they may have different errors.

Once you've gotten your copy, run by each item thoroughly.Make sure you have the necessary financial documents such as account statements, billing statements, and official receipts evidencing payments made on standby.Such documents will be your evidence or documentary support for disputing erroneous items on your credit reports.

Disputable Errors

When it comes to errors, you can pretty much dispute all kinds of errors on your credit report.An error is an error, regardless of the magnitude, extent, or impact on your credit report.You have the right to an accurate credit report that's as inviolable as the right to breathe, eat, or drink.But while you can dispute anything on your credit report, credit bureaus aren't required to investigate and correct all of them under laws that are applicable in their jurisdictions.

So what are the things on your credit report that you can dispute and compel credit bureaus to correct or cancel in your favor?In general, you can dispute items in your credit report that can't be objectively verified, and are outdated, incomplete, and inaccurate.Outdated information includes negative items such as bankruptcy, which can only be on your credit reports for a limited period of time.If you're living in the United States, bankruptcy can only appear on your credit reports for a maximum of 10 years while all other negative information can only be on your reports for a maximum of 7 years.So if your credit report includes your bankruptcy from 15 years ago, you can dispute that and compel the credit bureau that prepared your report to remove it from your current and prospective credit reports.

What are the other erroneous items on your credit report that you can dispute?These include:

• Balances or accounts that don't belong to you;

• Erroneous account balances and credit limits;

• Erroneous creditors;

- Erroneously reported statuses of accounts, e.g., current but reported as past due; and

- Timely payments that were erroneously reported as late ones.

The Dispute

After identifying errors in your credit reports that can be disputed with the credit bureaus that prepared them, you can choose from among 2 dispute options:by snail mail or over the Internet.

The Snail Mail Dispute

Disputing errors via regular mail can take a whole lot of time.So why should you still consider snail mail as a means by which to dispute errors in your credit report?Two words:paper trail.This can prove to be especially useful if for some reason your credit bureau's response to your dispute is delayed.

When talking about response or turnaround times for disputes, credit bureaus are compelled to complete their investigation and response within a maximum of 30 days from the time the dispute's been filed.The turnaround time can be extended to 45 days tops if you submit additional documentation to support your dispute after the bureau's investigation has already begun.In the United States, the law gives you the right to sue the concerned bureau for up to a thousand dollars if they fail to respond to you within the prescribed period.

If you decide to file a dispute via snail mail, ensure that your letter clearly identifies the information that needs to removed or amended and the reason or reasons why such information is inaccurate or outdated.Attach your documentary evidences that support your dispute such as statements of accounts and official receipts evidencing actual payments, among others.

When you send your dispute letter together with copies of documentary evidences, do so through registered mail.By doing this, you'll be able to obtain undeniable and uncontestable proof that you filed – and that they received – your dispute on a certain date from which the 30 or 45 day turnaround time will be based.And while waiting for the credit bureaus response, make sure you keep track of the processing time so that you can send them timely follow-ups.

The Online Dispute

If convenience is your thing, nothing beats filing your disputes online.You can do so from the comfort of your home and at your most convenient time.And more than just the convenience of filing disputes online, you can also check your dispute's status and receive the results online too.How cool is that huh?

Such comfort and conveniences have their corresponding challenges, however.One of them is that you will still need to send your documentary evidences via snail mail, which means you'll still have to go to the post office, the nearest mailbox, or the nearest courier service just to send physical documents to the credit bureau.

Another challenge you'll need to deal with when you choose to file your disputes online is that you will only see the results of the bureaus investigation and evaluation of your filed disputes online, i.e., you won't get a hard copy from them.This can be disadvantageous if you're required to present proof that the credit report used by a potential employer, financial institution, or utilities company that recently rejected your application is an erroneous one.

The Process

Once you file a dispute claim with the credit bureau that prepared your erroneous credit report, they can respond to it in a number of ways.It's possible for them to respond by immediately amending or deleting the information you contested.But if the credit bureau's able to verify the contested information later on, don't be surprised to find such information reinstated in your credit report.If the bureau eventually does that, they're obligated under the law to notify you of such reinstatement in writing.

As mentioned earlier, credit bureaus are generally mandated by law to respond to credit report disputes within a maximum of 30 days from the date of receipt, which can be extended to 45 days if additional evidences to support claims are submitted after investigations have already proceeded.And upon completion of investigations, credit bureaus will provide those who filed disputes with the results or findings of their investigation.They can even give free copies of amended credit reports if and when the disputes have been verified and effected in such credit reports.Even better, credit bureaus can be asked to formally send notices of corrections or amendments of credit reports to institutions that relied on such erroneous reports in deciding unfavorably on applications filed with such institutions.

Third Party Error

It's possible that the error in your credit report wasn't the fault of the bureau itself but of the source of their information, such as the bank you have an outstanding loan balance with or your credit card company.If the credit bureau's response to your dispute is that the error was verified as correct by your bank or credit card company, it would be in your best interests to go straight to the concerned institution and file the dispute directly with them instead.

Other Erroneous Credit Reports

If your credit report from one credit bureau happens to be erroneous, it's highly possible that your credit reports from other bureaus are also erroneous. Why? It's because they all get the necessary information from the same sources, i.e., your creditors.As such, it would be in your best interests to make sure that credit reports from other bureaus are accurate and free from errors too.

Documentary Evidence to Support Your Disputes

If you dispute certain pieces of information in your credit report with the credit bureau that prepared it, the burden of proof lies on you.You'll need to prove beyond reasonable doubt that such information is wrong and shouldn't be on the credit report.And as with court cases, you need documentary evidence to back up your accusations.

If your dispute relates to your personal information such as age, name, birthday, or social security number, then the obvious documentary evidences required for filing a dispute include copies of valid identification cards, copies of your birth or marriage certificate, and most recent billing statements.If the issue pertains to supposed "missed" payments, copies of cancelled checks or official receipts evidencing payment, or latest statements of accounts that reflect such "missed" payments should be sent to the credit bureau together with your formal letter of dispute.Just remember to send copies of the original documents and not the originals themselves, which should be in your custody at all times.

As mentioned earlier, you can expect a longer response time of 45 days maximum if you send additional documents after the credit bureau has already begun investigating your dispute claim.If you submit all documentary evidences upon filing your dispute, the maximum number of days in which the credit bureau's supposed to respond to you is only 30 days.

Chapter 15: Common Mistakes You Should Avoid While Repairing Your Credit

If you are thinking about repairing your credit, or if you are going through with the process already, there are some things that you should steer clear of. Here are some mistakes too many people make when attempting to repair their credit:

1: Disputing everything on your credit report

This book has already insisted that you shouldn't do it, as well as why it is a dumb idea. And yet, a lot of the time, when you hire a credit repair company, this is the first tactic they employ. It beats all sense that a "professional" opts for this route. For starters, it is absurd that everything in your credit report is inaccurate or erroneous. The credit bureaus base their reports on actual research. There may be several errors, yes, but the whole thing cannot be an error. By disputing the entire credit report, or having a credit repair company do it for you, you are making the credit bureau's work extremely easy- they will just toss out your dispute on the grounds that it is frivolous, and their case will easily hold its own in Federal Court.

2: Hiring a credit repair company

Reputation is everything and quite simply put, credit repair companies do not have a reputation for good results. As a matter of fact, the Federal Trade Commission, FTC, has been extremely critical of credit repair companies and here, you can see the FTC leveling one of their multiple fraud charges at a credit repair company that, on the outside, seems to be legitimate and effective in its services.

If you have had an experience with a credit repair company, you may have noted that the promises they make are often quite lofty. Ask yourself this- can these promises be fulfilled legally? Save your money and do the repair work yourself- it is as straightforward as it comes anyway.

3: Cancelling credit card accounts

Too many people do not realize that closing your credit card does nothing positive for your credit score. If you have a late payment on it that is dragging down your credit score, pay-for-delete is the way to go. Your credit score is reliant on the age of your accounts. When you close your credit card accounts and deal with new ones, it is very difficult to have a high score because of the young age of your new accounts.

4: Playing the balance transfer game

When you transfer credit card balances so as to avoid making your payments, you are only postponing the inevitable, while managing to make things worse at the same time. Consider that balance fees are added to your balance every time you make a transfer. You will only make your balance bigger and harder to pay, which will have very negative results on your credit score.

With what we've discussed in mind, let's now discuss some strategies you can use to boost your credit score by up to 100 points or more!

Chapter 16: The True Cost Of Negative Credit

In this chapter, you will learn that the adage of, "What you don't know will cost you" is more of a reality than one might think.Negative credit can eventually turn into positive credit, however while it is negative it comes with a cost.In the following paragraphs, I will be exploring the high cost of having a low credit score.

Most people don't want to be just another number, but the reality is you are in today's society. In times past, your social security number was the most influential number known to man, in its nine-digit form.However, there is a three digit number that is giving the social security number a run for its money, the infamous credit score.More companies and even individuals are looking at your credit score to discover your credit worthiness and your integrity.Never would the world imagine that three digits could stop someone from renting a home let alone stopping them from buying one.

Car dealerships have started advertising that your credit score won't get you denied from buying a car, yet after reviewing your credit report and score they will slap you with a 22% interest rate.So it won't hinder you from driving the car off the lot, as long as the Car Dealership profits a whole lot in the long run.The sad part is that it doesn't end there; it can also stop you from even getting employment...

Here is a credit riddle:

You go to the car dealership to get a car that you need in order to get to the job interview you just scheduled which is your dream job.The car dealership gives you the car with an interest rate of 22%.In addition, you have nowhere to live because every landlord rejects you instantly after looking at your credit.You then drive an hour for the interview to get to your dream job.Surprisingly, the hiring manger thinks you are very creative after glancing at your personal Facebook and Twitter page.However, he doesn't think that you will be the best fit for the bank vault supervisor position – handling millions of dollars.In retrospect, who wouldn't blame him because if your credit report shows that you can't be trusted with your own money, why would a bank trust you with theirs?So now with no job and no place to stay, you live in your car until they come to repossess it since you have no way of paying them back.Once again you are left with nothing…

Some may think that the above is fiction, when in reality the above riddle is reality to many people!!!

Who reviews your credit?

Below are the top individuals and companies that review one's credit in order to support their final decisions or outcomes:

Housing:

*Landlords

*Mortgage Lenders

Employment

*Employers

Insurance:

*Insurance Agents

Transportation:

*Car Dealership Lenders

The reason everyone on the above list checks your credit is because they believe that your three digit credit score is revealing you.They think that three numbers expose your ethics and your integrity.Below I will break down why your credit is so important within so many industries.

Housing:

*Landlords – Landlords know that renting is a temporary transaction, and the only way to establish some form of stability is to create a lease agreement for at least a year in most cases.All landlords understand that every tenant comes with their risk, but the greatest risk of all is the landlord not receiving rents from the tenant or worst the tenant leaving the apartment in shambles.Since the mortgage is in the landlord's name the tenant has no ties to the property outside the lease and can come and go as they please.With this in mind, a landlord will review a tenant's credit to see if their past will be a prediction of their future.

*Mortgage Lenders – Mortgage lenders, also known as underwriters, look at your credit worthiness.For example, their question is, is it worth giving you a $100,000 home loan when your credit report shows that you can't pay a $100 credit card payment on time?Underwriters don't care that you think once you become a homeowner, mysteriously, everything will change; they want to see the change now and the behaviors to be better now, before approving you.

Employment:

*Employers – If you step back for a moment you will agree with the employer's perspective.The principle is, you wouldn't trust someone to be over your millions in a vault if they could not manage their own finances.Honestly, you don't go looking for a person that never paid you back to lend them some more money, do you?

Insurance:

*Insurance Agents – If there were one word that is foundational to all insurance companies, that word would be – "RISK."

The Webster Dictionary defines Risk as:

The possibility that something bad or unpleasant (such as an injury or loss) will happen.

In the case of credit, your credit is reviewed in terms of the amount of financial risk that you bring to the table.The lower the score, the higher the risk!!!This truth is why a lower credit score results in a higher annual premium.Just in case you don't believe me, give your insurance agent a call...

Transportation:

*Car Dealership Lenders – Over the years I have had many clients debate me that

143

their credit could not be that bad because they are pre-approved for a car loan.They state they can go into any car lot and pick a car of their choice.Moreover, you might have that mindset also, however, I want to present two dangerous factors of why car loans are on a **level of their own**:

Dangerous Factor #1: Technology – Car Dealerships are slowly going away from hunting you down to repossess that brand new car you stopped paying for months ago.Now thanks to technology, they can track down and shut off your car from the comfort of their company.If you don't believe me, CNN did an investigation titled: "Pay up or your car engine will stop."

[Click here to read the full CNN article]

Dangerous Factor #2: Repossession Process – As covered in the previous chapter, if you don't pay, the collection process will favor the actual owners of the car, which is not you...

They know before you drive off the lot that if they don't receive any payments it will result in repossession, repossession can result in a judgment, and a judgment can lead to all your accounts being frozen.To that end, they don't mind you taking their car for a year-long "test-drive."

Overall, your credit can start impacting your life as soon as you turn the legal age to apply for credit.

Please Note: I want to ask for a moment of silence for those who started off with bad credit as a child because their parents put credit in their name without their consent.This strategy is very illegal, however, more and more parents with bad credit are doing it since times are getting a lot tougher.

In conclusion, I want you to remember that just in case you think your credit is too bad to look at, keep in mind – someone is still looking!!!

Points to remember:

*Negative credit can eventually turn into positive credit; however while it is negative – it comes with a cost.

*In times past, your social security number was the most influential number known to man...However, there is a three digit number that is giving the social security number a run for its money...

In the next chapter, I will go over the danger of being declined for credit.I will be explaining how one decline can cause a rippling effect...

Chapter 17: Ways You Never Knew You Could Raise Your Score

You can actually ask credit card companies to get rid of problems on your credit report even if you are actually in the wrong. What you want to do is simply call or write to the credit card company directly. Let them know that you understand you were late on a payment but point out your history and show that you have not been late in the past and you made a one-time mistake. (If you have been late frequently they probably won't work with you as much.).

Now if you have never made this mistake before or if you have rarely done it the credit card company may be willing to wave a late payment. This would mean that they take the late payment remark from your history and you may not even have to pay a fine. But by taking off the mark on your history they are improving your credit score. That one little late payment can be a big problem and it can result in your score taking a big hit. If it gets removed you no longer have to worry about it and your credit score could go up quite a bit.

Keeping old accounts open is another important way that you can improve your credit score. The oldest accounts that you have are actually improving your credit, whether they are positive or negative. What this means is you could have a long history of late payments with your oldest account but you're getting more positive marks on your credit from that account being so old than you are negative marks for the late payments. You don't ever want to close your oldest account unless you have no way around it. This account is doing great things for you.

Now if you have multiple accounts that are very close to the same age and one has a lot of negative marks you can close it. What you don't want to do is close the only account you have that's older than two years. (Of course, the older the account is the better it is for you.) Only close this account if there's an important reason for it or if you have another account that is very close to the same age and is giving you the same benefits when it comes to account history.

All those 'free quote' websites are actually hurting your credit score as well. You need to make sure that you are not signing up for a lot of those quotes. Even when you're searching for something like car insurance or health insurance you need to be careful. Free quotes may sound great but how do you think they're able to give you that quote? They need to know a little more about you in order to give you something that they can guarantee and that means they run your credit history and check out your credit score. That helps them to know whether you'll pay your bills or not and that affects your quote.

Pay your balance more than once a month. A lot of people use their credit cards for everything. That's either because it's easier to use instead of having to carry around a lot of cash, or because you just want to keep raking in rewards points that you can use for other things. Those are perfectly good reasons and if you're paying off the card every month you're not getting late charges or anything like that which is a benefit to you. On the other hand, you could be hurting your credit utilization rate.

Now you may be thinking, I pay it off every month so how could I be hurting my credit score? Well, when your bank or credit union sends you a bill they are telling you how much money you owe. That amount is also being sent to the credit reporting agency, which uses it to calculate your credit utilization rate. If your balance is $500 and you owe $500 then your utilization rate is 100% and that's going to look really bad on your credit report. It's going to lower your score by quite a bit.

What you want to do is make more than one payment per month. If your balance at the end of the month is lower than the limit then you're going to have a better utilization rate. The lower the rate you have the better it's going to look on your score, so make sure that you're paying as much as you can for each of your payments. That way, no matter when your credit card company sends in the balance owed, you won't get a big hit on your credit report and you'll be able to keep your score higher, where you want it to be.

Chapter 18: Ways To Repair A Bad Credit Score

It is time address a potential area of contention for some.That's right, this chapter will focus solely on how to fix a credit score is more bad than good.Maybe you are just now starting to look into what your credit score is like, and to your horror your credit score is not what you thought it was.Or perhaps instead you've run into some harder times recently, and your credit has taken a hit of which you're aware.Regardless of how you arrived at this point, having a low credit score has serious implications for other areas of your life (which we've discussed in previous chapters already).If you've already made the mistakes from the previous chapter and are stuck in a place from which you desperately want to escape, this chapter will provide you tips on how to do exactly that.

How Long Will It Take to Repair Your Bad Credit?

Knowing how long it will take to repair your bad credit can help to not only provide you with more knowledge but also scare you into not making these types of mistakes.For most types of actions that lead to bad credit, the transactions will be on your credit report for seven years.These actions include late payments, any repossessions that have occurred, foreclosures, short sales, and tax liens.The only category that will stay on your credit report longer than seven years is filing for bankruptcy.This type of misdemeanor will stay on your report for an entire decade.Understanding how long your credit history stays with you brings with it an awareness of how important it is to pay your credit off in a timely manner.The consequences, even when seemingly minor, have a historic trail attached to it that will be hard to shake for years to come.With this types of timelines in mind, let's take a look at the steps you must take if you want to improve your rotten credit score.

Step 1: Get Your Credit Report Transcripts

In order to begin cleaning up your credit, this first step is to get a copy of your most recent credit report.This report will give you exact reasons why your credit is in the toilet, and you need to pinpoint what is going on within this report in order to ever fix it.You don't have to pay any money to obtain these records.Through the Fair Credit and Reporting Agency, you are entitled to receiving a free copy of your credit report once a year.While doing this, it's important to obtain records from each of the major credit reporting agencies.This way you will be able to see how each type of credit reported is being perceived by the creditors that you choose.It's impossible to know which credit a potential will use, so you want all of these types of credit reports to be up-to-date.

Step 2: How to Clean Up Your Credit Report

Once you've gotten ahold of your credit reports, it's not enough to simply say, "clean them up".You need to know how to specifically make your credit report look more attractive.Let's take a look at how to do this now.

Tip 1: Finding the Mistakes

It might come as a surprise, but not all of the activity on your credit report is necessarily true.There might be mistakes.If there are, you need to dispute these claims.You will need to dispute this activity with the account that first put these charges on your account.To do this, you can either send a letter to the company in question or call their customer service line.These days, someone should be able to help you at most times during the day.

Tip 2: Dispute the Same Claims on Different Credit Reports

If you find that the same mistakes are apparent on different credit reports that you obtain, you will need to dispute each claim that is listed on the different credit reports.It's not enough to simply dispute one of the claims on one your credit reports, because these mistakes will still exist on the other reports that have been generated under your name.This can be tedious work, but it's worth it in the end.

Tip 3: Hire an expert

While you may have the wherewithal to figure out how to remove potential errors on your credit report on your own, you may not feel like going through the hassle of removing these inaccurate findings on your own.Credit repair companies and law firms do exist that will take care of these banalities for you.These companies are not allowed to promise that they can raise your credit score by any number of points.They will be up front and honest with you.If they're not and you feel like they're not a trustworthy source, find help elsewhere.

Step 3: Look for Positive Reinforcement

Secured credit cards, which we've already discussed, are specifically designed to help people who are having credit problems resolve their credit issues.Just because you've been denied certain types of credit because of your past actions, this doesn't mean that you're entirely out of luck.You have a chance to slowly repair your credit with this type of credit card opportunity.As with any card, you will have to develop better habits if you hope to revitalize your credit history.

Step 4: Be Consistent in Your Payment Amounts

It's important to avoid hinting that you are going through tough times or that you are experiencing financial trouble.To avoid this, it's important to in addition to paying your credit cards off on time, to also pay a consistent amount each month.For example, if you usually spend two hundred dollars each month on your credit card payments, and then suddenly you start to pay fifty dollars or even only twenty-five dollars, your creditors are going to notice. Be consistent in your payments so that your lenders don't worry.

Step 5: Places to Avoid Using a Credit Card

In addition to keeping your risk under control, you should also avoid using your credit card in certain places such as pawnshops or with divorce attorneys.These types of places indicate that you might soon be in a place of financial stress, and your creditors will deduct your credit score accordingly.

Chapter 19: Think Small

Early in my banking career a client came to me looking for a small, unsecured line of credit. She was a young woman in her early twenties with an irrepressible smile, the type of smile that makes you want to be helpful. Unfortunately, the smile wasn't enough. When her credit report came up I cringed. She didn't have a mortgage. She didn't have an auto loan. But she did have thirteen credit cards, all over their limit and many of them late.

"Is this right? It looks like you have 13 different credit accounts."

"Yeah!" She was very proud of her accomplishment. And at some level that makes sense. To have qualified for so many accounts she must have managed them well for a while, but clearly that time had passed. The lines had gotten the best of her, as they would almost anyone trying to juggle as many.

When I asked what they were for, she said that she'd always heard it was good to have multiple lines of credit, and she got great deals on clothes by signing up at the stores. She was correct about having multiple lines. The credit bureaus like to see a few lines being used, but 13 is just too many. Accordingly, her score was in the basement and she didn't qualify for anything, but I was able to provide her some direction for climbing out of her predicament.

We discussed setting money aside for her minimum payments and various strategies for attacking the debt. We discussed budgeting and envelope systems. But most important we discussed starting over as a borrower, and the importance of thinking small.

When it comes to acquiring credit there are countless seductions. The pull to add more and more is strong and comes from every direction.

It begins the moment we leave home. A 2009 study by Sallie Mae determined that

91% of college undergraduates have at least one credit card and over 50% of students have four or more. The average undergrad carries $3,173 in credit card debt. At a rate of 20%, these students are paying over $600 per year in interest just to maintain the debt.4

The marketing continues at our retail stores. A 15% discount at the register sounds like a smart move in the moment, but many retail cards come with poor rates and high fees. They are often exclusively for use at a single store. In addition, because of their tasty 'point of purchase' offers, it is tempting to obtain one at each of your favorite stores. Many of my clients have been shocked to see how many retail cards are listed on their own credit reports.

And through the mail it's obscene. Credit card companies send out an estimated 5.6 billion credit card offers per year. That's nearly 70 applications per household. Standing firm against this constant barrage of marketing is like keeping your footing in a rising tide. It's a challenge for anyone to say "no", especially if one believes, as many do, that more is better.

Remember, the credit card industry is not designed to keep us responsible. It is designed to sell us credit cards whether we need them or not, **resulting in...**

too many of us with too much debt on too many cards.

Don't get buried.

A safe number of unsecured credit lines is three. And frankly, if you are reestablishing yourself, two is sufficient.

Two cards, well used and well managed, are far better than any number overused and paid late.

But which ones do we choose?

If you already have a large number of credit cards and are scaling back your usage, ask yourself these questions:

Which accounts are oldest? Which accounts have been handled best? Do you have accounts tied to your existing bank?

Are your interest rates high due to past payment activity?

Longstanding accounts with a good history are rewarded by the credit scoring agencies. If you have an older account with a decent rate, it might be beneficial to try and keep it. However, if that account has a rate in the high twenties, make certain that they will lower your rate when you get the account back in line. They always can, but many are reluctant to do so.

If you're starting from scratch and want to limit yourself to just a couple cards, what should you look for? As a past banker I strongly suggest you **keep it personal**. Get to know the staff in your bank, including the Branch Manager, and apply for a card there. They may not have the best possible rates but being able to walk in and talk with someone face to face about your account is a powerful tool, and frankly one worth the extra interest.

Though banking is an increasingly automated industry, it never hurts to have an advocate with whom you can shake hands.

But what if you don't qualify for even one card?

If you are a new borrower or are trying to rebuild your credit it's quite possible you won't qualify for any unsecured debt. If this is the case, consider **secured cards**. A secured card can be an excellent tool when you're in this predicament.

Here's an example of how they work: You provide $300 to the bank as a security deposit. In return, they issue a credit card to you with a limit of $300. You still have to make regular payments and manage the account as you would any other.

At this point a good question would be "Why would I put up my money just to use the bank's money, especially when I'm going to be paying fees and interest to do it?" The reason is simple: a secured card can help you build positive credit history.

That is its most important purpose and is why you still have to use it responsibly!

Then, after a year or two of positive use, ask to replace it with a standard credit card. It is a small step, but a smart one.

Small steps in a safe direction are far better than great leaps into oncoming traffic!

Another strategy, often considered, is to get a **joint card** with someone who has good credit. This can be very effective, but is also dangerous!

The benefit is that you are often able to get a card with better terms than you could on your own. The danger is that, should the card be misused by either party, the credit of both owners is impacted. Having witnessed the fallout of this too many times, I cannot enthusiastically promote it. Yet, I admit if managed with care opening a joint account can be a successful tactic.

However you choose your cards, resist the temptation to apply for too many. Your credit score will suffer and worse, the challenge of effectively managing a larger number of accounts is an unnecessary risk.

Recommendations to help you **Think Small:**

1. Remember, the credit card industry exists to sell credit, not to benefit you.

2. Choose your accounts wisely. Prioritize longstanding accounts, personal relationships and decent rates.

3. If possible, establish a personal relationship with your local bank. It is always to your benefit to be recognized as a person rather than an account number.

4. Two or three is plenty for anyone.

Chapter 20: Increase Your Score 60 Points In 30 Days

First of all, the title of this chapter is possibly an oversell to some while very achievable for others. Whether you can do this or not depends on the status of your credit at this time. If you have bad credit it will probably take more than 30 days to fix. If you have excellent credit then you may already have the highest score possible for you.So let's make sure you know how to maximize (manipulate) your credit score no matter where it is today.

The first thing we will need to know is what your score is today. Youwill not get a score from www.annualcreditreport.com. In order to get a score, you will have to pay for it, from each bureau, or you can get them for free from some of the free credit websites such as;

www.creditkarma.com™

www.creditsesame.com™

or others.

These are important since they will update your score monthly and keep tabs of how they have changed.

Once we have your score you will want to look over your credit report to make sure it is accurate (see chapter 5).

Finally, we will do two things that are easy to do for long term gains and that take a short time to accomplish. It may require you to spend money.

The first thing to do is to look at your revolving accounts (credit cards, gas cards, store cards, etc). In order to have the best score possible, these accounts should have a balance due **that is no more than 30% of their limit**. This means that if card "A" has a limit of $ 1,000 you should not owe more than $ 300 on that card. If you have the cash to pay these down then do so, if you do not have the cash then maybe you can pay the debt down on credit card "A" by using credit card "B". But follow the same rule for card "B".

Example:

Card "A" has a limit of $ 1,000 and balance of $ 550

Card "B" has a limit of $ 1,000 and balance of $ 100

We need to bring down the balance of "A" to $ 300, so we need $ 250. Card "B" can be increased to $ 300 and we only owe $100 so we can use $ 200 of it to pay down card "A". Now both cards are at 30% of their limit. You can accomplish this by paying card "A" online with card "B", by asking card "B" to pay down card "A", or with a courtesy check from card "B". Please note that these transfers usually have fees charged. Consider these fees in your calculations.

Make sure that you have at least 3 revolving accounts that have a small balance owed. Why is it important to owe money? Your score is a snapshot of your credit. Imagine if you were in school, were an excellent student, knew the subject forward and backwards, but never turned in any homework. What kind of grade would you get? If all of your revolving accounts are paid off the credit scoring system cannot tell whether they have been paid off for years or whether you paid it off last month. A big part of your score is how timely you pay your debts. This means you have to have debt. If all your bills are paid off, go charge up the cards a little and do not pay them off. Now if you don't care about your score and want to increase it when you need it, then you can have everything paid off until you want to increase the score. Just remember that it will take 30 to 60 days for your lender to report your new balance to the credit bureaus, so plan accordingly.

The second thing we will do is take care of any negative items on your credit report. Follow the instructions in Chapter 4.

If you find this too complicated or would like a professional assessment, please go to our website,

www.fix-my-score.com,

and sign up for our personal consultations.

Chapter 21: How You Can Build Good Credit And Get Rid Of Your Bad Credit At The Same Time!

We all want to build good credit – it's important to do so because it is an essential part of life.It not only helps us to buy a home, or be in a good and stable position with our finances but it also allows us to obtain a loan easily should we ever need it.

However, it is so important, vital even, to establish your credit and have good credit if not for now but for your future.What is more, it is vital that you do fix your bad credit. What can you personally do?

I realize that I am being very repetitive here, but really, there is no fast way of fixing your credit! Anyone that says that you can fix bad credit in a few days or weeks is a liar.

Build Your Credit Slowly but Effectively

The first thing that you need to do is to get your household bills in your name.If you really want to establish a better form of credit, change who the main bill payer on your utilities.

Big utility companies send out information and bills to your home and even though it might not seem much, putting your name on your bills is important.If your partner has a good credit already established, ask to change them to yours.

You can actually build your credit by simply having the utility bills in your name and paying them on time every month!Yes, it is that simple, though of course, things aren't going to change overnight, it takes time but even slow progress is worth a lot.

Always Pay On Time

An important part of establishing your good credit is to ensure you keep paying those bills.Try to avoid late payments; if you have to, set up reminders when the payment is due and if you can, avoid underpaying — that is worse than paying late because companies may choose not to accept anything less than full payment.

If you want to remember yourself, you could actually set up a payment system so that your bills come out of your account automatically.This can be a really great way of building your credit of paying history and help to avoid missing payments as well.

For some bills, such as your credit cards, you should try to pay at least the minimum amount each month.If you have extra money, put it towards your credit cards, however, if you are struggling, pay the minimum at least.This way you avoid a late payment and avoid adding more interest.

Credit card companies hate when you miss a payment, they would rather take what you can afford than nothing!What is more, if you miss a payment, you could incur a penalty which adds more to your debt.

Try to avoid going over your balance on each credit card also.You don't want to max out on your cards; it might not look too great on your credit report.If potential loan companies see you have maxed out several high balance credit cards, they might decide you are not worth the risk.Instead, try to pay at least half of the balance off before adding any more balance to it.

This helps you to avoid going over your limit and helps to keep bad credit away from you also.Of course, you can end up going over your limit on some months but if you do, try to repay the amount back as quickly as possible to keep the credit effect low.

You could even get a store card from a certain store you shop at often.It could be an electrical store or food store, but whatever it may be, make sure you use it.You put a balance on the card; you repay it back at the end of the month.

This can also be a fantastic way to fix some bad credit because you can show a pattern of good history of repaying your items off.Even if it is a small local store, it can all count in the long run.

Stay In Regular Employment

Depending on what type of loan you may be going for, lenders will take account of a lot of things including your employment record.Of course, it would be ideal to keep a job at all times but to be honest, unforeseen things can happen.You can lose your job or have your hours cut back.

However, if you can, stay in regular employment.This will look good on your credit report because it shows that you want to work and have the means to repay back a loan should you get one.

If you change work every few weeks or months, creditors are not going to like that!They may think that you aren't a good risk because you keep changing jobs which means that you might be out of work and cannot repay back the loan they offer you.

However, if you have a good long term employment history, that can look well on your credit.In the creditor's eyes, you have the means to support yourself and have a way to repay back money as well.You can become a good risk because stability is what creditors look at.

 What is more, this can help you when it comes to getting a loan in the future and even a mortgage.If you are freelancing or self employed then that can go for and against you.It really depends on how much you work and how much you earn.If you only work a few hours each week then the chances are your credit can be affected by this.

If you are self employed however and have a good steady flow of work then you might find that your credit is good.Even if you have bad credit because of your past employment record, it can become a lot better when you have a good and stable period of employment.

Use Installment Loans

 Installment loans can be fabulous to help get your credit from being bad to good.These allow you to take out something say a car loan for how many years and repay the loan back.

You have set payments for these loans every month and you can really establish your credit.What is more, if you have had trouble in the past with loans, these types of loans can really help you to build on your credit and make it good again.

Avoid Moving Around Too Much

If you can, stay in one home and avoid moving around too much.If you do, it can often be reflected on your credit report which could effectively hurt it.You move around too much and you are considered to be a risk, if you stay in one location you are less of a risk.

It might sound crazy to you but actually this is what creditors look at.It all counts and if you want to get rid of that bad credit and replace it with good credit, you need to try to stay in one location.Not easy at times of course but it is worth a try.

Improve On Your Existing Credit Scores

You see your credit scores now and they might not be too good, however that doesn't mean to say they can't be again!You can turn your bad credit into good, it can be improved upon so don't ever say it can't because it can.

So, one way in which you could do this is to apply for a credit card.However, you don't want to be too hasty and choose just any; you want to choose a credit card that offers the best deal for you.You want a low interest rate card as well as maybe one which can offer you some cash back when you purchase items.

Don't apply for a new credit card – you want to stick to existing cards you have if possible.Though, if your credit is at a fairly good place, you could look to applying for a new credit card but be careful over what you are getting.For every credit application you make, it will all go against your credit so make sure you only apply to the suitable option and one that you know you will be accepted for.

Remember, if your application is denied, it will go against you credit as well, so be very careful.

Have a Savings Account

If you can set up a new savings account.This never hurts especially when it comes to showing potential lenders that you have a few accounts with your bank open.Even if you only add a few dollars each week, it still can look good on your part.

What is more, if you have a savings or even a checking account, your bank may be willing to offer a credit card in the future.However, don't open four or five accounts just to build credit, that doesn't look good, it's really bad so just open one savings account.

Have Debt – Keep It Low

Having debt is bad and it will be on your credit report also.This is going to be tough to get rid of but it's important to keep paying this off.You want to try to keep repaying each debt you have no matter how old it may be and keep the overall debt low.

If you keep adding to your debt, it will only get worse for your credit.You really do want to try to keep your debts low so that you can keep control over it and manage it easily.

Don't Be Afraid To Ask For Some Help

If you are struggling with some repayments, try to get them lowered.You can always ask for the payments to be lowered, it might not always work but you never know.You could be able to get a debt stretched out longer for a period of time and the payments can be lowered as well.

Give Your Bad Credit Time to Heal

There are going to be times when you feel as though nothing is working.However, your bad credit isn't going to go away just like that.It is going to take time so you do have to give your good credit time to kick in.

Eventually your bad credit will turn into good credit and it will reflect on your credit report as well.What is more, you can use some simple tricks about building your credit including using your credit card to make smaller purchases rather than using cash.

You could charge small everyday items to your credit cards in order to help build your credit.Though, you don't want to place big ticket items on there and be left struggling to repay these, instead you can put all of your gas charges on to the card.Just avoid the bigger items like electronics.

If You Can, Pay More

Minimum payments are good when you are repaying your credits off.If you have a lot of credit cards to pay, you need to try to at least pay back the minimum amount.If you can, pay a lot more!

Making more payments can reflect better on your credit.It is also a great way to slowly reduce the amount of debt you have as well.

Stick Below Your Credit Limit

To be honest, it will be very wise to try to keep below your actual credit limit!Now, most people do go over their credit limits and as such, it reflects on their credit.It can be bad especially if you struggle to repay the money owed so you really do want to try to keep within a good limit.

Your credit cards are a net – your safety net, but that doesn't mean you should use it for anything and everything.You should try to use them only when you need to.If you go over your limits, you will end up getting more bad credit.

Check Your Scores Every Year

An important part of changing your bad credit and making it good again, is to keep check on how well your credit scores are.If there is something you aren't too sure of, then dispute it.

This can be a simple way to upping your credit scores.

Have Debt – Spread Them Out

Having one huge balance on one credit card can actually be very damaging to your credit score; it can look very bad indeed.However, if you can spread out your debts from one card to several then it can look much better.

It's not a sure fire way to actually make your credit greatly improved but it can help it a lot.

Chapter 22: Dealing With Professional Credit Help

Credit repair is big business, and there are many companies that will promise to help you get out of bad credit problems.There are a number of legitimate resources that can help you in improving your credit score but there are also a number of less than reputable companies out there that will take your money but offer you few (if any) valuable services.A few basic tips will help you see the difference:

Tip #34: Seek professional help If you are in over your head, and your credit is so bad that you cannot get a loan and may even be facing bankruptcy, you may want to seek help from professionals.There are a number of financial professionals that can help you with credit repair:

Bankruptcy lawyers and bankruptcy advisors : Bankruptcy lawyers can help represent you in bankruptcy proceedings.Advisors can help you decide whether to apply for a bankruptcy and how to proceed once you do decide to file.

While getting a bankruptcy lawyer and filing for bankruptcy can be upsetting and can dramatically affect your credit score for many years, it can also give you a chance to start over financially and can help you reestablish good credit again in the long run. Credit repair companies and credit counseling companies: These companies can help you by acting on your behalf with credit companies, by advising you on what you can do to repay your bills faster, and by helping you make better financial decisions. Accountants and tax services: Accountants and tax filing services can help you make the most of your money by making sure that you do not end up overspending on taxes. Bankers and bank officers: Most banks today want to not only help you keep your money but are willing to work with you to make the most of it.As a banking service, many banks today offer free investing advice, saving advice, and personalized meetings with bank officers that can help you figure out your money situation. Lenders and bad credit lenders: How you deal with lenders will determine how well your credit score works. Avoiding too many inquiries by not applying for too many loans, establishing long-term business relationships with bankers, and doing business with bankers in an organized and professional way (i.e. paying your debts on time) will go a long way towards giving you a credit rating.In turn, a good credit rating will make it easier to deal with lenders.

Tip #35: Look out for credit repair companies. Many companies out there advertise that they can help you with credit repair, but the quality of these services - not to mention what they offer - varies widely.Some companies really can help you with credit repair while others are actually under investigation for suspect business practices. If you decide to seek help from a credit repair company, be sure that the company is legitimate and offers you viable services.

In general, you should be looking for non-profit credit counseling services rather than credit repair companies (some of which are really just lenders offering home equity loans anyway, which are of limited use to you if you want to improve your credit).

Check to make sure that the company has good standing with the Better Business Bureau and clients who are happy with the credit repair services they received from the company.Always read the paperwork carefully before you sign and make sure that you understand how much you are paying for and how much you are paying.

Before deciding to seek help from a credit help or credit counseling service, be sure that the problem cannot be resolved on your own.Indications that you may need credit counseling include:

-You cannot pay your bills and avoid the necessities of life.

-You avoid the phone, the mail, and the door because you are being harassed by collection agencies.

-You have avoided going out because you feel terrible about your financial state.

-You have no idea how you will repay your bills and loans - you do not know where to start.

Tip #36: Seek free or inexpensive help before seeking paid credit repair help If you need credit repair, odds are good that your finances aren't in the best possible shape.That likely means that you should attempt to spend as little as possible on credit repair - the money you save can be channeled into repaying your debts.Before seeking credit repair services, follow the tips in this ebook in order to repair your own credit.

Also, seek out free or inexpensive sources of credit repair help.Some non-profit credit counseling services are actually registered charities and will work on your behalf.If you can get help from one of these companies or undertake credit repair yourself, you will be able to save money quite easily.

In addition, these companies tend to be more legitimate than credit repair companies that take your money, anyway.

Tip # 37: It will be easier for financial experts to help you if you seek credit repair help sooner rather than laterIf you do decide to seek credit repair help from the experts, it makes sense to seek that help before your financial situation spirals too far out of control.After all, credit repair experts can do little for you if your credit and financial situation is so bad that the only option left to you is bankruptcy.

Tip #38: Look out for credit repair scams There are a number of credit repair scams out there.These scams often promise to help free you of bad credit, when in reality the "experts" offering these services will either overcharge you, involve you in illegal activity, or actually put you in a worse financial situation.Look out for these most common scams:

1) Credit repair companies that tell you to lie on loan applications or suggest that you develop a second identity.This is illegal

and dishonest. If a company suggests that you open accounts in a new name or falsify your information on loan applications, run, don't walk, away.

You can be charged with fraud for doing this - and you will be held responsible for your actions, even if you were acting under the company's advisement. You certainly don't want to add legal troubles to your credit woes.

2) Credit repair companies that charge you fees or hidden fees for things you could do for free yourself - such as work out a budget. Also be wary of companies that ask for money up front.

3) Credit repair companies that promise to pay your creditors from money you pay to them and which they keep in an escrow account. This is a common scam and it presents a huge problem for the debtor.

Here's how it works: the debtor gives money to the credit repair company, presumably for paying off debts. The company places the money in an escrow account where it grows. The idea is that the company will eventually pay off your debts when the amount reached in the account matches the debts.The problem is that in the meantime, the credit repair company is removing some money from the account for administrative fees while creditors are becoming more and more anxious, increasing the interest on the debts and even starting legal action against the debtor.This type of "credit help" can actually ruin your credit rating!

4) Credit repair companies that pressure you, don't listen to you, or want you to sign a contract you have not read. Such companies are not to be trusted and should be left well enough alone.

5) Companies that offer you fast or instant credit repair - no matter how bad your credit.This is simply a misleading a claim that no company can legitimately deliver on.If you have very bad credit, it may take years to fully repair.

In many cases, these companies will claim that they can remove your poor credit history from your credit report by disputing it.This is false information. You simply cannot remove true and accurate information from your credit report.It is true that a credit bureau must investigate a claim of inaccurate information within thirty days, but this does not mean that the company will automatically remove the information.

In fact, if the information is accurate, the data will stand.Credit bureaus are aware of this common credit repair scheme and have become very good at detecting it.Many credit repair companies (and even some individuals) will try to dispute every ding on a credit report, hoping that the backlog of disputes will cause the credit bureau to automatically remove the offending items from the report (the credit bureau is legally required to remove disputed items it has not investigated within 30 days).This technique is a scam and is dishonest since you are not disputing inaccurate information.

Refuse to do business with credit help companies that use this practice.

6) Companies that don't tell you your rights or try to take money for things you could do yourself.You can get copies of your own credit reports and have the errors on them fixed for free yourself - a company that does not tell you can do this yourself ifs taking money form you for things you can easily do yourself.

It is a dishonest practice, and companies who follow such business practices should be avoided at all costs.

Also, if a company does not advise you of your credit rights, then that is an indication that they are not really on your side in the first place.Why would you want to do business with a company that does not help you?

Tip #38: Get a good team on your side to help you with your credit score A good team of professionals can help you get your credit score back in shape.Your most important member of your team is yourself - you are the one with the financial agency and (with this ebook) the knowledge to become your own best advocate in credit repair.Besides this, you may want to check with your local library for financial help books.You may also want to include financial experts such as credit counselors or others to help you.If you decide to seek a team of experts to help, be sure that you check each person's credential, standing with the Better Business Bureau, and past clients to make sure that the person or company can really help you.Beyond this, make sure that you sign a contract or agreement with each professional member of your team.

Tip #39: Your bank has good and reliable credit information One free and professional source of credit information is your bank.Your banking officer may be able to offer you a great deal of professional, free advice, especially as banks are trying harderand harder to provide good personal services to customers.

Your bank may also have a number of credit solutions - such as overdraft protection - that can help you keep your credit in good repair. Banks are realizing more and more that many of their clients are dealing with less than ideal credit.Banks are trying to meet the demands of this new group and can actually be a powerful ally for those who are trying to improve their credit.

Chapter 23: How To Remove Negative Marks From Your Credit Report?

There are also ways to remove any negative marks on your credit report aside from the dispute of legitimate errors. These steps have to do more with the use of negotiation skills and personal relationships. These steps are made possible because while credit agencies are obligated to verify the data they receive, the lenders are not required to report their lending activities to the credit reporting agencies.

1.Request for a goodwill adjustment. This is a more personal approach that you require to make towards your creditors. You may write what is called a goodwill letter. It is essentially a letter seeking for compassion towards removing from your file any past delinquencies. Find the name of your creditor or the one in charge of your accounts; tell him of your reasons behind the late payment. It can be because of a temporary unemployment phase, an unexpected expense because of an illness or accident, a death in the family or any reason that can tug at their emotions. Use the term "goodwill adjustment" instead of "remove" or "delete."

Here is a sample of a goodwill letter:

Your Name
Your Address
Your City, State Zip
Date
Company Name
Company Address
City, State Zip
Re: Account Number
To Whom It May Concern:

I've enjoyed being a customer of Bank A since 1995. Today, I'm writing to request a goodwill adjustment to my credit files.

I was a model customer from the time I received my credit card in 1995 until 2006, when I suffered a medical illness which wrecked my finances and my ability to make timely credit card payments. As a result, I fell behind on my payments by 60 days. Fortunately, I was able to turn my financial situation around and I've been timely with my payments ever since.

I'm preparing to shop for a mortgage and was told those late payments will keep me from getting the best interest rate. I'm requesting a goodwill adjustment since the payments do not reflect my current payment status. Thank you for your time reading this letter and the consideration you've given my situation.

Sincerely,
 Your Name

This letter can be found at: http://credit.about.com/od/creditrepair/q t/Sample-Goodwill-Letter-To-Remove-Negative-Credit-Report-Information.htm

2. Give and take. You can also negotiate with your creditor for an exchange on their removal of your negative records on their next report to the credit agencies. For example, you can offer your creditor

to enroll your loan in an automatic payment scheme using your debit card. This way you are showing him that you are committed to pay and you only want your credit report to mirror your improved financial decisions. You can also make other offers such as restricting your loan in such a way that the creditors will have an advantage but in return, they will omit your negative records on their reports.

3. Pay in full. If you have the funds available, you can even make the deal sweeter to your creditor. In exchange for the removal of your negative records, you are willing to pay the entire amount. This is called a pay for delete offer. Make sure to keep it writing and request both a confirmation of receipt of your letter and a signed agreement of your creditor to your offer.

Here is a sample of a pay for delete letter:

Your Name
 Your Address
 Your City, State Zip
 Collector's Name

Collector's Address
Collector's City, State Zip
Date
Re: Account Number XXXX-XXXX-XXXX-XXXX
Dear Collection Manager:

This letter is in response to your [letter / call / credit report entry] on [date] related to the debt referenced above. I wish to save us both some time and effort by settling this debt.

Please be aware that this is not an acknowledgment or acceptance of the debt, as I have not received any verification of the debt. Nor is this a promise to pay and is not a payment agreement unless you provide a response as detailed below.

I am aware that your company has the ability to report this debt to the credit bureaus as you deem necessary. Furthermore, you have the ability to change the listing since you are the information furnisher.

I am willing to pay [this debt in full / $XXX as settlement for this debt] in return for your agreement to remove all information regarding this debt from the credit reporting agencies within ten calendar days of payment. If you agree to the terms, I will send certified payment in the amount of $XXX payable to [Collection Agency] in exchange to have all information related to this debt removed from all of my credit files.

If you accept this offer, you also agree not to discuss the offer with any third-party, excluding the original creditor. If you accept the offer, please prepare a letter on your company letterhead agreeing to the terms. This letter should be signed by an authorized agent of [Collection Agency]. The letter will be treated as a contract and subject to the laws of my state.

As granted by the Fair Debt Collection Practices Act, I have the right to dispute this alleged debt. If I do not receive your postmarked response within 15 days, I will withdraw the offer and request full verification of this debt.

Please forward your agreement to the address listed above.
Sincerely,
Your Name

4. Wait. Time heals all wounds, even financial ones. Take advantage of the 7 year statute of limitation of your negative records or 10 years if you have filed for bankruptcy. Charge offs take seven years and 180 days. Student loans, paid taxes, foreclosures and lawsuits are also dropped after seven years. While waiting, if you make better financial decisions, you can improve on your score as you wait for the seven year period. In fact positive records can average out your negative records that will result to a higher credit score even before the 7 years elapse.

Conclusion

For some, being debt-free can seem like a pipe dream. However, everyone can be debt free with careful planning, diligent money management, and goal setting.

Everyone has the right to financial freedom and security. By developing a healthy relationship with money by developing your financial blueprint and protecting your finances by limiting debt you are well on you way to a bright future, for you and your family.

The road to becoming debt free may seem like a long and bumpy one, but the skills you've learned in this book, it should be easier than you thought. It may take baby steps at first, but keep in mind that every journey starts with a single step.

You have already taken the first step by reading this book and making the conscious decision to take control of your finances!

Thank you and good luck!

* 9 7 8 1 9 9 0 0 8 4 7 6 8 *